CW00351055

YOU'LL
NEVER
WALK
ALONE

Also by Rachel Kelly

If: A Treasury of Poems for Almost Every Possibility (co-editor)
Black Rainbow: How Words Healed Me: My Journey Through Depression
Walking on Sunshine: 52 Small Steps to Happiness
The Happy Kitchen: Good Mood Food (with Alice Mackintosh)
Singing In The Rain: 52 Practical Steps To Happiness
– An Inspirational Workbook

YOU'LL NEVER WALK ALONE

Poems for life's ups and downs

Chosen and introduced by
Rachel Kelly

First published in Great Britain in 2022 by Yellow Kite
An imprint of Hodder & Stoughton
An Hachette UK company

1

Copyright © Rachel Kelly 2022

The right of Rachel Kelly to be identified as the
Author of the Work has been asserted by her in accordance
with the Copyright, Designs and Patents Act 1988.

Internal illustrations © Shutterstock.com
For Poetry Credits, Copyright and Permissions see page 218

All rights reserved. No part of this publication may be reproduced, stored
in a retrieval system, or transmitted, in any form or by any means without
the prior written permission of the publisher, nor be otherwise circulated
in any form of binding or cover other than that in which it is published and
without a similar condition being imposed on the subsequent purchaser.

A CIP catalogue record for this title is available from the British Library

Hardback ISBN 978 1 529 39534 1
eBook ISBN 978 1 529 39535 8

Typeset in Krete by Goldust Design

Printed and bound in Great Britain by Clays Ltd, Elcograf S.p.A.

Hodder & Stoughton policy is to use papers that are natural, renewable and
recyclable products and made from wood grown in sustainable forests. The
logging and manufacturing processes are expected to conform to the envi-
ronmental regulations of the country of origin.

Yellow Kite
Hodder & Stoughton Ltd
Carmelite House
50 Victoria Embankment
London EC4Y 0DZ

www.yellowkitebooks.co.uk

For Katherine

Contents

Introduction

Words can be a way to make sense of our feelings, a role poetry has played for me ever since I was a small child engrossed in a large, illustrated anthology in the corner of the school library. *You'll Never Walk Alone* is my attempt to convey something of this personal enthusiasm. My hope is that poems can become part of your emotional life too, even if hitherto you have never felt that poetry was your thing.

Poetry helps my own psychological wellbeing in two main ways. First, it makes me feel less alone. Through poetry we discover other people who have experienced similar sentiments, and we are not solitary in our despair or indeed our delight. When we have a poem by our side, whether on a bedside table or tucked into a bag, it feels as if we are accompanied by a friend: an authorial arm is wrapped around our shoulders.

I know this lovely sense of companionship that poetry bestows, not just from my own personal experience, but also from running poetry-reading groups in schools, charities and prisons for the last eight years. This work began after I published a memoir entitled *Black Rainbow: How Words Healed Me: My Journey Through Depression*, in which I described how poetry had been my friend when I fell ill in my thirties with severe depression and subsequently recovered. The results I saw, and the way that people were helped, convinced me of poetry's power to keep us company. Hence this book's title and why I have become something of an evangelist for the role poetry can play in our wellbeing at a time when many of us feel isolated. Yes, you can share your feelings with friends, or a therapist if you are lucky enough to have one. But that may not be possible. Sharing words as an alternative allows us to become more connected to ourselves and others (not least the poets themselves), and this has never been more true or necessary than during our uncertain times.

A second emotional benefit of poetry, I've found, is that it gives us permission to feel deeply, whatever mood we might be experiencing. Neurologists say that poetry speaks to a primitive part of our brain, perhaps a part that was more active when poems were passed down orally before writing was invented. You know when someone asks how you are feeling, and you say 'fine'? When you are not feeling fine at all. But it feels scary to admit how you really are. And that can be true even if you are on top of the world.

Sometimes in the past, I have kept my feelings repressed, for fear of being overwhelmed – even positive feelings, as if too much joy might unbalance me. It's safer that way, isn't it? Not to reveal your heart. Showing our feelings makes us vulnerable, doesn't it? And we British, traditionally, prefer what used to be called a stiff upper lip. But shutting down our passions is also sad: a life lived in dreary black and white when it could be experienced in technicolour.

And sometimes it is downright dangerous to stay buttoned up, not to acknowledge the truth of what we really feel, especially feelings that we don't really allow, like vulnerability or anger. I remember a doctor once telling me that depression could be considered a case of 'anger turned inwards', something I pondered when I fell ill myself,

Well, this anthology is an invitation to let rip, be that in grief or joy. To yell from the rooftops. To shout for unalloyed happiness. Or to wallow in utter despair. All emotions are allowed and welcome within these pages. It's all okay here. What we resist, persists.

Expressing our feelings allows us to acknowledge them in their full and glorious reality – and move along if we need to. And that's another way that poetry helps. Because it doesn't just give expression to your feelings, it changes them too – usually in the direction of greater wellbeing and general expansiveness.

Instead of feeling tensed up, you feel more relaxed – because poetry doesn't work on your nerves or your brain, but on your heart and your feelings. Poetry is your friend in dealing with all this emotional stuff. Knowing that someone else has felt in a similar way makes it all okay. Poetry allows all those feelings to find expression. It lets us more fully inhabit that feeling. And gives us the words and images for our emotions when we struggle to find them, which is especially good if you are no wordsmith or are busy with other things, as most of us are. Poems are short, and handy when you are in a rush and trying to nail a mood. There's that lovely moment of recognition when you go, 'yes! – that's spot on! *That's* what I'm feeling!' The poets in this anthology refresh my own stale vocabulary. They are so generous in sharing amazing images to make sense of our moods, images that have made my frightening feelings less scary, and my happy feelings even happier.

My choices are texts not just about words that can console or comfort us, and those around us – though they often do this too. Rather I am drawn to poetry that allows us to enjoy a full range of emotions. As George Orwell didn't say, all feelings are equal, and no feeling is more equal than others.

All our different moods are valid, important, and what make us human. I sometimes think our mental health might be better described as our emotional health. Allowing and experiencing all my emotions is something that has taken me years to achieve, and poetry has helped me through every step. Rather than fight or reject our feelings, we may be calmer if we just allow them all to exist and accept them, becoming more attuned to and aware of our inner emotional lives.

This selection has plenty of cheery poems, but also darker ones to reflect the messy emotional reality of our lives. I have organised my selections according to the season in which they more or less 'belong': we have seasons of our minds, be they wintry and dark, or more spring-like and hopeful. Connecting the time of year to our human experience is a way of acknowledging the importance of allowing all our feelings, negative and positive. It happens in nature! It's okay! Nature does not deny the presence of struggle, or joy, or loss, or gain, or darkness, or light. All are part of the natural cycle of life. The metaphor encourages us to embrace all our feelings: to find opportunities for growth. No experience is ever without value. We thrive when we can accept the ups and downs in our emotional life – when we work with them, rather than against them.

Poets have long connected the time of year to our human experience. We need only think of Shakespeare's opening line, spoken by the Duke of Gloucester, in *Richard III*: 'Now is the winter of our discontent / Made glorious summer by this sun of York.' In the nineteenth century, Keats writes in his poem 'The Human Seasons': 'Four Seasons fill the measure of the year; / There are four seasons in the mind of man: / He has his lusty Spring... He has his Winter too of pale misfeature.' Here Keats relates our inner transitions to the outer seasons.

I have followed his example in organising this anthology: a mood can be expressed by a seasonal image. Using nature as an emblem for our emotions feels appropriate. Winter does feel like a time of abandonment and retreat; Summer, a time of joy.

Why has this seasonal metaphor endured as a dramatic and poetic device, and as a way of conceptualising our personal ebbs and flows of achievement, happiness, grief and hardship? It is one that humanity cannot seem to dismiss or surpass, even though many of us now no longer live close to nature, and the seasons no longer frame our lives in the way they did in a more agricultural age.

Understanding nature to understand ourselves may have been helpful to poets because it reminds us of various emotional truths: first, that our feelings constantly change, just as the seasons can change with bewildering speed. Psychological change is needed and is inevitable. However bleak or desperate our mood, this feeling is subject to change, just as the seasons change. Nothing ever stands still, or maintains its current state, identity or shape for very long. In fact, just as nature cycles through seasons of change and transformation, effortlessly and naturally, so do humans transition through mutating psychological states.

This is as true for happiness as it is for sadness. The joy you experience during your summers will not last for ever. There will inevitably come a moment when you move into another season, which may lead to pain and anguish. Yet this, too, is only temporary; and this too will eventually pass.

We need these changes. The cycle of the seasons brings the contrast that makes life interesting. Without darkness, we could not enjoy light. Even those who live in warmth recognise the need for at least the symbols of the cold. Without change, half of the keyboard of life would be missing: no flats or sharps, on a piano with no black keys.

Using nature as an emblem for our emotions reflects a second psychological truth: that our feelings are often complex and nuanced, sadness mixed with elation. Even in the darkest moments, there are flashes of joy. Complete and unalloyed sorrow is as impossible as complete and unalloyed joy. There is a term in botany

– vernalisation – referring to seeds that can only thrive in Spring if they have been through the severity of Winter. The two are held together in a hidden wholeness. It is one of nature's paradoxes.

Nowhere is this paradox more evident than in Autumn. Leaves wither and fall; it is only by shedding its leaves that a tree can survive the windy and sun-deprived Winter. Expending energy on leaves that won't soak up much sun is no longer viable, so this way trees conserve resources; sudden gusts could also blow them down if they still had all their leaves to catch the wind. The shedding of the tree's leaves, sad as it may seem, is for the sake of the life of the whole tree. This paradox is expressed by Charles Mackay in his poem 'Oh Ye Tears': 'The rainbow cannot shine, if the drops refuse to fall; / And the eyes that cannot weep, are the saddest eyes of all.'

There's a final, third way I've found connecting poetry to the time of year helpful: the way it echoes the truth that our feelings grow and alter over time, akin to the way that trees and flowers grow and alter. We too are part of the natural world: unfurling, becoming the fruitful and inevitable outcome of what we are naturally meant to become.

The seasons thus offer us a means of understanding the importance of surrender, of letting go, of trusting in an intrinsic and slower-paced process of reaching our potential. Understanding nature in this way allows us to release ourselves from struggle and speediness, and the need to become our best instantly, without journeying through several unique stages. We can abandon the sense that we are battling against our circumstances. The invitation instead is to rely upon an innate sense of timing – nature's sense of timing.

The naturalist and poet Henry Thoreau often philosophised on the benefits and inspiration of living in harmony with the seasons. In 1853, he wrote: 'Live in each season as it passes; breathe the air, drink the drink, taste the fruit, and resign yourself to the influence of the earth.'

Yet most of us don't heed Thoreau's advice or take nature's example. We tend to want the dramatic weight loss in a week; the job promotion to be offered today; the grief that binds us to someone to untangle and release its grip on our hearts quickly. We do not see the benefits of a season of emotional depletion and reflection. We do not see that this sets us up for a dramatic personal rebirth when the time is exactly right. Unlike our most primal and humble example, the natural world, too often we wish for instant gratification.

Given that all seasons can be nurturing, this anthology, accompanied by commentaries illustrating how each poem evokes a mood or feeling, begins with Winter. Spring and Summer follow naturally, and the book ends with Autumn, when your poetic appetite may turn to something more reflective. Our own emotional realities may not follow such a linear journey. We might one moment feel a Winter sadness, and the next something altogether more joyful, akin to the elation of Spring. Taking whatever season matches your mood, readers will find a lyrical companion present as a guide to those feelings, whether your need is for comfort in sadness or how to pin down the elusive nature of happiness.

'Winter' addresses suffering, offering words for anguish when you may not be able to articulate your emotions to others, or even perhaps to yourself. 'Spring' has poems that bring the first glimmer of an inner optimism: these texts can shift our way of thinking, with words of innocence and rebirth. 'Summer' contains more outward-looking readings, turning to nature as a way of helping us to re-engage with life. It is also a season of love, with parallels easily drawn between fertility and the fecundity of the earth. 'Autumn', the final section, naturally has a harvest feel, representing a gathering in of emotional riches for the months ahead. There are texts for squirrelling away, full of wise counsel in readiness for the coming Winter, as well as memories of the seasons that have passed.

Arranging poems about our moods in this seasonal way is how I organise my own 'Healing Words' poetry groups. These workshops grew out of my own lifelong enthusiasm for poetry as something that keeps me company through life's peaks and valleys, ever since that moment in the library at primary school. It all began when I was even younger, thanks to a poetry-mad mother who encouraged me to read poetry books as an even smaller child in the same way that other parents share their love of baking or football. My favourite anthology was *The Golden Treasury of Poetry*, selected and with a commentary by Louis Untermeyer. Inside its front cover I wrote: 'This book belongs to Rachel S. Kelly January 8th 1976.' For the avoidance of doubt I added a bookplate on which I inscribed 'Rachel Sophia Kelly' in turquoise italics.

A second favourite anthology was *The Golden Journey: Poems for Young People*. I learnt Edgar Allan Poe's 'The Raven' from its pages. And as a teenager I particularly cherished the edition of *The Rime of the Ancient Mariner* my mother gave me one birthday, with its swirling studies of the sea by Gustave Doré. A leather-bound *Oxford Book of English Verse* was a present as I left for university.

I've been banging on about the healing power of poetry for a while now, but I was forced back to the poetry drawing board around three years ago, when my mother died. She always used to say 'go deeper' if in doubt. For me that means you've got to pick a poem or two. Which is what I've been doing over the last few years. This time round, going deeper means not just poems for the tricky times, but poems which let you experience joyous feelings more deeply too. My mum's death taught me that life is too short not to.

In retrospect my luck, I think, was not to be frightened of poetry, something I now realise may be the case with many who feel verse is not for them. Partly this is because I have never studied poetry, and don't therefore associate it with passing exams or having a 'right' or 'wrong' reaction to the words on the page. I read History at university, not English Literature, so I have an eclectic, personal view of what I should or shouldn't like, or what is supposedly good or bad poetry. My enjoyment is almost a physical one in the sound of the words, the way they speak how I feel and unlock how I feel in a bodily way. Sometimes there is almost an electric shock of recognition when I read a poem: the hairs on my arms will stand on end, as if the energy radiating off the page connects with my own energetic field. If there is no reaction, no connection, or the language is too highly wrought or the allusions too incomprehensible, I simply move on to the next poem that does connect with me. Please feel free to do the same.

I have found that poetry has always been there for me as I have navigated each new experience, be it heartbreak (captured in Pele Cox's poem 'Afterwards,'), or a moment of unexplained joy that catches you out in an unexpected place (conjured in 'A Blessing' by James Wright). It awakens something inside me that has lain dormant, the sort of feelings that can vanish with the normal run of everyday life but, the poem reminds us, are still inside us.

Poems are also there for us for the kind of shock that comes on with other critical moments in our lives, be it a parent's death, or your own illness. This was especially true for me when I fell ill with depression. I wasn't well enough to read a chapter, let alone concentrate on a whole book. Instead, I derived comfort from soothing poetic one-liners, ones that told a more positive story and reminded me that I was not alone. Poets are generous: they give us the words when we can't find them. Research suggests I am not the only one.

Studies agree that bibliotherapy can have a role to play in treating mental illness, though this is a relatively new area of research. I loved coming across a study saying that elderly people who read live an average of almost two years longer than those who don't pick up a book.[1]

I enjoy interacting with these kinds of inspiring messages in my everyday life by keeping them close, literally. The French philosopher Michel de Montaigne used to write his own inspiring quotations on the beams of his sitting room, where they remain today. I do not have any beams to decorate, but I like writing out quotations in nice ink in a tidy script, perhaps decorated with an illustrated border. I like short poems, and copying them out helps me remember them. Feelings are awakened during the process of committing the words to the page. Writing slows you down and gives you time to learn the lines. I learn what the poem is made of – each word and pause and line feels special. Its meaning is one that has become part of me. It works its cathartic magic.

Typically, this is something that happens in my poetry work-shops. Not always, and not for everyone. But sometimes we have shared a poem that pierced to the heart of someone's immediate circumstances or psychological state, which can make for emotional scenes. I remember one woman beginning to cry as she read Derek Walcott's poem 'Love After Love' at a meeting which was held at my local hospital under the auspices of a mental health charity for those finding life difficult. As her trickle of tears became a torrent, we were spellbound as we waited for her to regain her composure. 'I feel

---

[1] In September, 2016, researchers from Yale University School of Public Health studied 3,635 people aged over fifty, and found that book reading 'provides a survival advantage' among the elderly of twenty-three months. The more people read, the more likely they were to live longer.

understood,' she said eventually, and we in turn all understood what she meant. She had, in Walcott's phrase, struggled to 'love again the stranger who was your self'. The poet's compassionate invitation to: 'Sit. Feast on your life' was the invitation she needed, in language that spoke to her, to imagine loving herself in a way she had found so hard. Poetry had worked its magic, unlocking and allowing her feelings in a new way.

What began as a personal collection has become a stockpile of poems and passages that resonate with many of the hundreds of people I have been lucky to work with and get to know. Those poems which moved only me have been discarded; what remain here are those texts to which plenty of others responded. (We meet for four sessions, one for each season. A small bunch of around fifteen of us gather for an hour or so, during which we share six or seven poems and texts, selected for their power to heal or inspire. In turn, different group members read aloud a poem, if they wish, and then we discuss our interpretation of the poem, how it relates to our lives, and how it might be helpful.)

They are poems that, commonly, people find of use whether they are in despair or feeling elated. As Scott Fitzgerald wrote of literature: 'You discover that your longings are universal longings, that you're not lonely and isolated from anyone. You belong.'

I am confident that you will connect with some of my selections. I have never set out to look for the poems and passages. They have always sprung up naturally from what I was reading, the main criterion being that I felt impelled to stop and write them down. They grabbed me, as the best poetry always does, because they resonated so strongly with my emotional reality.

My hopes are that I am imparting some texts you might otherwise have missed. Above all, by writing introductions to my selection of poems, I hope I have shared my enthusiasm in a way that amplifies yours. I warmly invite you to be my companion, as I metaphorically take your hand. I benefited from reading poetry in this way with my late mother – all those years ago – whose own excitement and belief in poetry infected me. My aim, ambitious as it sounds, is to make you feel that we are reading the poems together, with me by your side. My reactions may arouse your own. Perhaps your experience of reading the poems will also be enhanced by reading about the lives of the poets at the end of the book, where you will also find some thoughts on how to enrich your enjoyment of poetry, whether that is reading it, writing it, or memorising it. We will be, I hope, partners in feeling poetry's power.

I am conscious that some readers may struggle with a few poems in this selection that celebrate the link between nature and the divine. In the 'Summer' section, for example, E. E. Cummings explicitly thanks God for his creation of natural beauty, as does Gerard Manley Hopkins. Religious poets like R. S. Thomas often use nature as a metaphor for the rebirth and revival of their faith, and the resurrection of Christ. But non-religious readers may also seek inspiration from scenes of nature's restoration and regeneration. All of us require the strength to overcome major adversity at some or many points in our lives. We hope that through trauma and adversity we can re-emerge; that after the metaphorical Winter, we will experience a bountiful, fresh Spring. So, while many readers will not feel themselves to be religious, perhaps my chosen writers, despite their religious convictions, may still feel relevant.

I hope you can draw upon the resource of experience in this diverse collection and find you feel the same kind of emotional peace that these poems have brought me. If some poems, on first reading, seem difficult to relate to, I suggest looking at them simply as a way individuals have used language to the best of their abilities to pass on their insights. Doesn't that seem a little less daunting?

A last thought to encourage you. While it is easy to know what anger or joy or sadness is, many of us find it hard to *tell* what it is. That is what the writers in this anthology have done for us so variously. Accept their gift and let their words nurture you in unexpected ways.

Rachel Kelly, London, August 2022

WINTER

Time for Sadness

Introduction to Winter

Winter is the darkest point of the year. The first three pieces included in this section are similarly bleak and hopeless. It is too late for the character in Smith's poem: he has already drowned. The night burns on for Fitzgerald and is lingering and torturous, a nightmare where all hope is gone. In Berryman's poem, only emptiness is left. In these pieces, there is no comfort to be had at all, no possibility of escape.

Despair is often linked with thoughts of death and desertion, and the next six pieces also speak from that darkness. The sense of agony is acute in Lincoln's letter, terrifying in Hopkins and Clare. While Clare suffers from having been abandoned by his friends, Cox evokes the cruelty of a misogynistic lover. And in 'Sometimes I Feel Like a Motherless Child' we feel the heart-wrenching tragedy of the forcible separation of children from their parents by slave traders. In *The Desert Fathers*, desperation descends into exhaustion and lassitude. Yet in each of these texts there is also hope: a yearning for, and possibility of, escape. The promise evoked in these first poems grows towards the end of the Winter section. In the final few pieces the voices are still those of the lost, but they have found a shred of belief, and they are clinging on to it. For Sexton and Goethe, this comes from having faith, trusting in something greater. For Doshi, it is a sense that we are being listened to; for Keats, that melancholy is something we do well to accept, rather than being defeated by it.

Where, then, can we find any comfort among these dark poems

and thoughts? Primarily, by allowing our own darkest feelings to find expression, and thereby some sense of ease. We can feel into our own darkness, which counterintuitively relieves it.

And there may be relief in realising that others have been desperate too. Berryman's first wife Eileen Simpson remembers a time when the poet Galway Kinnell met a woman who carried around a copy of 'He Resigns' in her handbag.[2] On being asked why she would carry around such a desolate poem, the woman explained that she had discovered it when on the brink of suicide, and finding someone else who had felt the same emptiness as she had brought her such comfort as to save her life.

The difficulties we face have echoed through the generations and across the globe. You are, temporarily, part of a community that has suffered, and beneficiary of a kinship that transcends the limits of time and place. There's something comforting in that.

Even when describing the most difficult of times, through the gloom of these texts there are flashes of promise and touches of optimism. The poets are throwing a lifeline out at sea: the words give you something to hold on to.

 These writers have succeeded in expressing their experience of sadness with such extraordinary skill. However bleak that time was, and unwell they were, they found the courage and imagination to record their ordeals. To me, these acts of creation feel like symbols of hope and a triumph of the human spirit over any anguish. These texts can also be useful on a practical level, to explain to someone else how you are feeling. It may be impossible to beat the descriptive language of some of our greatest writers. They provide the most astonishing written record of the reality of suffering.

---

2 This anecdote comes from the preface of the 1990 edition of *Poets in their Youth*, by Eileen Simpson

1. 'Not Waving but Drowning' by Stevie Smith

Nobody heard him, the dead man,
But still he lay moaning:
I was much further out than you thought
And not waving but drowning.

Poor chap, he always loved larking
And now he's dead
It must have been too cold for him his heart gave way,
They said.

Oh, no no no, it was too cold always
(Still the dead one lay moaning)
I was much too far out all my life
And not waving but drowning.

The first lines shock us with their stark message from a man who died by drowning but speaks to us, moaning from some afterlife. In the next two lines, the drowned man continues to speak, his tribulations unnoticed and misunderstood by those around him.

In the second verse, a new voice is introduced: that of the glib, uncomprehending observers, who imagine that the man's death has been caused by a straightforward heart attack brought on by the cold, when his agony is mental, not physical. They take at face value the idea that he was a jolly chap, always larking about: in fact, he was what doctors call a 'smiling depressive' whose illness is especially deadly as it is not easily apparent to others. Both voices in the poem are linked by the repetition of 'ing' in waving, drowning, and larking. The word 'cold' is repeated too, but is different in each use, reflecting the two conflicting voices.

The voice of the drowned man returns in the third verse. He emphatically contradicts the onlookers, explaining 'it was too cold always'. His words are unbearably poignant because we long for him to be waving but know – now really know – that he was drowning, and it is too late for us to help.

We are left reflecting on those in our own lives who seem to be coping but are struggling; and what those lines may be telling us about ourselves as well: pretending to a jollity we do not feel, possibly for our entire lives, and with potentially fatal consequences. This poem encourages me to be more emotionally honest and open about my real feelings when I feel 'much further out' than others may realise. It's an invitation for you to share your true feelings too.

2. From *The Crack-Up* by F. Scott Fitzgerald

Now the standard cure for one who is sunk is to consider those in actual destitution or physical suffering – this is an all-weather beatitude for gloom in general and fairly salutary daytime advice for everyone. But at three o'clock in the morning, a forgotten package has the same tragic importance as a death sentence, and the cure doesn't work – and in a real dark night of the soul it is always three o'clock in the morning, day after day.

Fitzgerald says that easy daytime platitudes and strategies to lessen our gloom don't work in the middle of the night. Different rules apply. The usual cures are redundant. And for those who suffer, it feels as if time has stopped at three o'clock in the morning. It is always that hour. It is impossible to ever enjoy the relief of daytime's perspective, 'daytime' having a different and finite feel to it, compared to the endlessness of night-time suffering. In a final image, which has become commonplace, the reality of the darkness of the night and the darkness of our soul merge into one, into a 'dark night of the soul'.

So why do daytime approaches to suffering not work at night? Fitzgerald nails the problem in another memorable image. Lying in bed, the minor hassle of a 'forgotten package' manages to seem as important as a 'death sentence'. At night, when we are 'sunk', we lose all sense of proportion or the ability to judge what really matters. In short, we have lost our way. More frightening still, Fitzgerald suggests, that inability to assess or appraise the seriousness of this all-encompassing gloom extends to fill every waking hour.

Fitzgerald's analysis of profound mental anguish reflects his own serious ill-health and his struggles with alcoholism by 1935, when he was in his late thirties. Here he contemplates his inability to distinguish between the trivial and the important. He wrote that he gradually weaned himself off 'all the things he used to love' until 'every act of life from the morning toothbrush to the friend at dinner had become an effort'.

Though now recovered, I suffered two severe depressive episodes in my thirties, as I mentioned in my introduction. Fitzgerald's words remind me never to judge my dark thoughts in the middle of the night, as well as being the most brilliant shorthand for what depression can feel like: that it is three o'clock in the morning, all the time.

3.   'He Resigns' by John Berryman

Age, and the deaths, and the ghosts.
Her having gone away
in spirit from me. Hosts
of regrets come & find me empty.

I don't feel this will change.
I don't want any thing
or person, familiar or strange.
I don't think I will sing

any more just now;
ever. I must start
to sit with a blind brow
above an empty heart.

Here's a paradox: a poem that manages to convey a sense of being and feeling nothing, despite the poet's inevitable use of words, which are something. A hollowness is evoked using short words, and short sentences, with only the odd image ('hosts of regrets') and adjectives (the 'blind' brow, the 'empty' heart), as well as the simplest grammatical constructions and verbs in the first person.

An emptiness also comes from the repetition of the word 'don't': so, we have 'don't feel', 'don't want' and 'don't think'. Berryman has given up on nuanced language, just as he has given up on his grown self and all he has experienced through his life: 'the deaths, and the ghosts'. He is even indifferent to 'Her having gone away / ... from me' – perhaps referring to a past love, which, along with 'Hosts of regrets', finds him 'empty'. I remember reading this poem soon after my mother had died – 'Her having gone away / ... from me' and finding it unimaginable that I could be impassive in the face of such a loss. But Berryman's nullity does not allow for any feelings at all.

He pares his vocabulary down bleakly to the bone, just as he himself has been pared down. He is hollowed out with nothing linguistic to offer, just as he has nothing emotional to offer, other than sitting with a 'blind brow', blind here meaning lacking perception, and judgement. His normally extremely active and reliable (and scholarly) equipment has let him down and is no longer working. Meanwhile, 'above an empty heart' repeats the word 'empty' from the first verse for emphasis.

The word 'ever' seizes our attention in the last verse, after the unnerving and only semicolon in the poem makes it sit alone at the start of the line, with nothing to distract us from its finality. We are suspended in the purest state of loss: a purity that, in a second paradox, lends a richness and beauty to Berryman's nihilistic vision. He allows us to be open to our own pain.

In the end, Berryman's own pain proved too much for him. This poem is taken from his final volume, *Delusions, Etc.*, published in 1972. The work was already with his publishers when its writer ended his own life, jumping off a bridge onto the banks of the frozen Mississippi.

But the poem has saved the lives of others, as I recounted in the introduction to this section: the story goes that a woman carried a copy of the poem around in her handbag, as she said that finding someone else who had felt the same emptiness had stopped her taking her own life. When unwell, I remember being asked how I felt, and finding it impossible to articulate the emptiness inside, other than by shrugging my shoulders. But I could share Berryman's poem.

4. From a letter to John T. Stuart, 23 January, 1841, by Abraham Lincoln

For not giving you a general summary of news, you must pardon me; it is not in my power to do so. I am now the most miserable man living. If what I feel were equally distributed to the whole human family, there would not be one cheerful face on the earth. Whether I shall ever be better I cannot tell; I awfully forebode I shall not. To remain as I am is impossible; I must die or be better, it appears to me.

Lincoln suggests that there are only two paths available to him – death or recovery – with an unswerving certainty that these are his only options, and death is the more likely outcome. He cannot continue as he is.

He conveys the strength of this conviction in two ways: first, his assertion that he is now the most miserable man alive in the whole world. The placing of the word 'now' is poignant. It is as if there were a process by which we could decide who was the world's most desperate person at any one point, and that Lincoln has qualified for the position. Second, he evokes the sheer vastness of his melancholy by saying he has enough sadness to wipe the smile off every single human being who is alive in the world. This belief that there are only two paths open to him contrasts with his own uncertainty about whether he will ever 'be better'.

Here we see that even a man as great as Lincoln had flawed judgement when it came to his own health. He predicts he is likely never to recover, though history tells us otherwise: a reminder that we are not always our own best judge, and that we are sometimes more pessimistic than we need to be.

That was certainly my case when I despaired of my own return to mental health. Each time I fell into depression, I was convinced that recovery was practically impossible. Like Lincoln, I remember thinking death was more likely. I wish I had known, when I was very unwell, that the future president was equally uncertain that he would get better. It would have introduced me to the idea that even the greatest among us can misjudge the future. And that when we are ill, we cannot easily imagine being well again.

The fact that such a giant of a man could have lived not just to tell the tale, but to continue to such prominence, prompts us to remember that pain can pass.

5. 'No Worst, There Is None'
by Gerard Manley Hopkins

No worst, there is none. Pitched past pitch of grief,
More pangs will, schooled at forepangs, wilder wring.
Comforter, where, where is your comforting?
Mary, mother of us, where is your relief?
My cries heave, herds-long; huddle in a main, a chief
Woe, world-sorrow; on an age-old anvil wince and sing –
Then lull, then leave off. Fury had shrieked 'No ling-
ering! Let me be fell: force I must be brief.'

O the mind, mind has mountains; cliffs of fall
Frightful, sheer, no-man-fathomed. Hold them cheap
May who ne'er hung there. Nor does long our small
Durance deal with that steep or deep. Here! creep,
Wretch, under a comfort serves in a whirlwind: all
Life death does end and each day dies with sleep.

T.S. Eliot wrote in his essay on Dante's work that genuine poetry communicates before it is understood. When we first read this poem, we can let the words wash over us. Even if we do not necessarily instantly understand exactly what Hopkins means, we can feel his despair. He evokes the unending, unrelenting nature of that despair with the unforgettable image of a mind having mountains – cliffs from which we fall. Repeating the word 'mind' in a grammatically odd way makes the phrase more striking still. The terrible twist is that we never reach the bottom. The sense of unending pain is established in the first line 'No worst, there is none'. He uses 'worst', not 'worse': there is no end to this depression, and no point at which he can reassure himself it won't get any worse. His pleas to 'Mary, mother of us, where is your relief?' and 'Comforter, where, where is your comforting?', though addressed to the Blessed Virgin and the Holy Spirit respectively, stand out for their child-like simplicity, like a small infant appealing to their parents, repeating the word 'where' to stress their desperation.

We experience the jerky, jumpy sounds in lines such as 'More pangs will, schooled at forepangs, wilder wring' (once a particular form of agony is established, its return is even worse). The unsettling effect is amplified by the poem's broken rhythms in a line such as 'My cries heave, herds-long; huddle in a main, a chief / Woe' and the way the word 'lingering!' itself lingers as it is stretched out over two lines.

The images tear at our own hearts. The poet's pain feels like being beaten on an anvil, causing him to cry between the intermittent blows. Of all the extraordinary ways Hopkins finds to divulge the depth of those feelings, for me the most extraordinary is that image of the mind having chasms down which we fall. It is one that allows someone who has not known despair – 'hold them cheap /

May who ne'er hung there' – to feel something of that descent into dizzying horror. (I remember that same feeling of falling when I was depressed.) Our hearts go out to Hopkins even more when we realise that he wrote the poem in the 1880s, while experiencing severe depression himself.

Hopkins was conflicted throughout his life. He loved natural beauty, but became a member of the Jesuit Order who, as a method of self-abnegation, averted their eyes from beautiful things. He was gay but took vows of chastity. Even his religious beliefs themselves were a source of inner turmoil requiring sacrifice: converting to Catholicism meant severing ties with his family, Victorian society, and many of his peers, all of whom were High Anglican. For a man who had already sacrificed so much for his faith, the loss of that faith would have been as terrifying a prospect as his poem suggests.

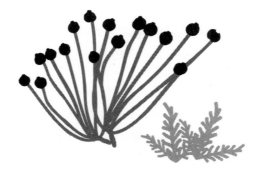

6.   'I Am' by John Clare

I am: yet what I am none cares or knows,
   My friends forsake me like a memory lost;
I am the self-consumer of my woes,
   They rise and vanish in oblivious host,
   Like shadows in love's frenzied stifled throes
And yet I am, and live – like vapours tost

Into the nothingness of scorn and noise,
   Into the living sea of waking dreams,
Where there is neither sense of life or joys,
   But the vast shipwreck of my life's esteems;
And e'en the dearest – that I loved the best –
Are strange – nay, rather stranger than the rest.

I long for scenes where man hath never trod,
   A place where woman never smiled or wept;
There to abide with my Creator, God,
   And sleep as I in childhood sweetly slept:
Untroubling and untroubled where I lie,
The grass below – above the vaulted sky.

Clare attempts to affirm his own existence with the solidity of his opening 'I am'. But instantly we learn that no one cares, or even knows that he still exists, that his loneliness is about his lack of connection with others even more than his lack of connection with himself. He speaks so plainly that it takes a moment for us to realise the horror of what he is saying. His use of the word 'none' is devastating in its certainty and simplicity: he has lost all his links with others for whom he is a distant memory. Partly this alienation is the fault of his friends, who have forgotten him. (As a poet from a poor rural background he was celebrated, but also exploited and treated as a sort of performer by his patrons and smart London society in general.) But partly he is to blame. He is the only person who is preoccupied by his own troubles, which shadow his hitherto loving relationships. Meanwhile his own physical existence dissolves into 'vapours', his physical reality disappearing into a nihilistic dream world.

In the second verse, his own estimation of the extent of his utter brokenness is brought to life in the image of the 'shipwreck' of his mind. Then he reveals that, most poignantly of all, those who were once closest to him are now more alienated than those he knew less well, an alienation that many who have suffered from mental illness will recognise.

By the last verse, Clare has given up on others in this life and longs for escape to the next. He wishes to be apart from any other human being, alone with grass, sky and his creator. He wants to return to how he slept as a child, to a place where he will no longer be tormented by the loss of the men and women he had once been connected to as an adult. The only safe portion of his life was his childhood when he could lie 'untroubled' asleep on the grass, a yearning that is all too familiar to anyone who has known insomnia as an adult and marvels at how they slept easily when they were young. This sense of nostalgia for happier, worry-free times fits well with the easy rhymes and ballad-like feel of the poem.

There's something moving about Clare, the great poet of nature, best known for his exquisitely precise images of the outside world, here describing an aspect of interior psychological sadness: his alienation from others and the depression that led to years in an asylum. While he was there, he was prescribed an experimental cure: observation of the natural world. I find this poem affecting for another reason. I was lucky enough to be supported by my family and friends when I was unwell, and I cannot imagine how I could have survived without their love and help. Clare, like many others, was not so blessed.

(As in all of Clare's texts, which were frequently edited – without his approval – to make them metrically 'smoother' and more acceptable to literary good taste, there are variants of this one.)

7.   'Afterwards,' by Pele Cox

he says,
It would be good
to find a woman as bright
as me.
She uncurls, thinks:
not unlike burial,
lying here
before light comes.

The room so black
a charcoal smear,
their limbs bare.
Him, her,
ash, bone,
a cigarette
and where on earth
to go from here.

The poem's title 'Afterwards,' with its unexpected comma, reads as its first line. This gives the feeling that we are already in the middle of the poem; spectators arriving after the action. We do not really know what is going on. We feel as if we are spying on the lovers, barging into an intimate post-coital scene. We feel even more uneasy because we instantly hear something cruel said out loud that was not meant for us, and we do not know why it is being said.

The seemingly innocent, reflective tone of the *'It would be good / to find a woman as bright / as me'* which is not italicised, unlike the rest of the poem – as if discussing a sensible romantic strategy on which we can all agree – amplifies the line's true brutality, devastating both for the intellectual arrogance of the speaker and the casualness of his rejection of his lover.

The woman herself takes a moment to respond. We wait, shocked at what we've unwittingly heard, as the female lover 'uncurls' herself, adjusting physically to this new reality. Only in the next line do we understand that she too understands fully the unkindness and finality of what has been said – it is as a body blow, as good as a death sentence – 'not unlike burial'.

The woman's emotional reality is reflected in the room's bleakness. What should be filled with images of post love-making warmth and bliss is drained of any colour or light, just as charcoal is wood burnt to blackness. The imagery is ambivalent. A post-coital cigarette becomes dangerously confused with ashes or even human remains; human limbs become worryingly close to the bones of dead bodies. In a few taut words and images, Cox conjures up the exact moment and feel of heartbreak, and the bewilderment that follows the collapse of an entire cosmology. But in her acknowledgement that the relationship is over, we can take some hope, a hope first hinted at in the first verse with its line 'before light comes'. The darkest moment is just before dawn.

8.   'Sometimes I Feel Like a Motherless Child' by Anon

Sometimes I feel like a motherless child
Sometimes I feel like a motherless child
Sometimes I feel like a motherless child
Long way from my home.

Sometimes I wish I could fly
Like a bird up in the sky
Oh, sometimes I wish I could fly
Fly like a bird up in the sky
Sometimes I wish I could fly
Like a bird up in the sky
Closer to my home.

Motherless children have a hard time
Motherless children have such a hard time
Motherless children have such a really hard time
A long way from home.

Sometimes I feel like freedom is near
Sometimes I feel like freedom is here
Sometimes I feel like freedom is so near
But we're so far from home.

What if we cannot rely on the one person who supposedly will always be there for us, our mother? This African American spiritual, which would traditionally have been sung by enslaved people, conveys the desperation of that sense of utter abandonment.

The first three lines have a child-like repetition about them, as if a lonely kid were rocking themselves to sleep. The verses, given their origin, naturally have a sing-song quality to them and do indeed roll off the tongue. There is an inkling of hope in the word 'Sometimes': a reminder that we do not always feel so motherless. Although this plaintive lament can be interpreted literally, referring to the horror of the breaking up of families by separating children from their parents, it might also be metaphorical. The motherless child could be yearning for his or her African homeland, each verse ending with the word 'home'.

This idea is developed in the second verse, in which the writer longs to fly 'closer to my home'. Repetition adds to the plaintive feel of this cry from the heart. The third verse suggests quite how tough the experience is of being motherless: it is 'hard'; 'such a hard time'; and 'such a really hard time'. In the last verse, that word 'Sometimes' again suggests the possibility of hope.

Yet the spiritual achieves its power by juxtaposing the longing for freedom, and the desire to be reunited with home in every sense, with the finality and utter desperation of the last line: 'But we're so far from home'. And, despite all this suffering, at no point does the writer call for retribution.

Nothing compares with the experience of enslaved people. But all of us can feel motherless at times, even if we are blessed with the most loving of mothers. In my darkest hour, my mother could not comfort me – she who had hitherto been able to soothe any pain. There is, it turns out, a limit to a mother's ability to succour her child.

It was something my own mother recognised: it was she who gave me this poem. Now a mother myself, I too sometimes feel powerless in the face of the suffering of my own children. This spiritual allows me to accept my own limitations, just as it may have helped my own mother to accept hers.

9. 'Accidie' from *The Desert Fathers*, translated by Helen Waddell

When this besieges the unhappy mind, it begets aversion from the place, boredom with one's cell, and scorn and contempt for one's brethren, whether they be dwelling with one or some way off, as careless and unspiritual minded persons. Also, towards any work that may be done within the enclosure of our own lair, we become listless and inert. It will not suffer us to stay in our cell, or to attend to our reading: we lament that in all this while, living in the same spot, we have made no progress ….

Towards eleven o'clock or midday it induces such lassitude of body and craving for food as one might feel after the exhaustion of a long journey and hard toil, or the postponing of a meal throughout a two or three days' fast. Finally, one gazes anxiously here and there, and sighs that no brother of any description is to be seen approaching: one is forever in and out of one's cell, gazing at the sun as though it were tarrying to its setting: one's mind is an irrational confusion, like the earth befogged in a mist, one is slothful and vacant in every spiritual activity, and no remedy, it seems, can be found for this state of siege other than a visit from some brother or the solace of sleep.

The opening sentence refers to the effect of 'Accidie' or 'acedia' besieging the mind. The word comes originally from the Ancient Greek 'akedeia', and means a lack of care, or indifference, and is often translated as the 'noonday demon'. This extract describes, with psychological acuteness, warmth and self-deprecation, a different aspect of despair: a longing for distraction, combined with a listlessness rather than an acute agony. Here the condition is diagnosed by one of the Christian monks, many of them hermits who became known as the Desert Fathers and who lived an isolated life dedicated to contemplation of the human soul, in the Egyptian and Syrian deserts around the third to seventh centuries AD.

You get the feeling the author is gently laughing at himself. He paints a picture of his own contradictory feelings. One moment he has only scorn for his brethren. The next, he is darting in and out of his cell, on the lookout for a fellow monk, and any old monk will do. By the end, he would even welcome 'the solace of sleep' to relieve his noonday demon.

What consolation can we draw from the Fathers? Perhaps the knowledge that the monks who knew the dangers of acedia nonetheless kept going to the desert. They courted the challenges of the noonday demon in the hope of strengthening themselves for further work.

You might imagine their challenges are a far cry from those confronting us in the twenty-first century. Yet many of the symptoms they describe have modern-day parallels: I for one am quick to blame anyone or anything but myself for my own inertia, whether it's my office – 'boredom with one's cell' – or my unimaginative colleagues. How reassuring to realise that such complaints are as old as time and we are less different from our forebears than we might like to think.

10. 'The Sickness Unto Death' by Anne Sexton

God went out of me
as if the sea dried up like sandpaper,
as if the sun became a latrine.
God went out of my fingers.
They became stone.
My body became a side of mutton
and despair roamed the slaughterhouse.

Someone brought me oranges in my despair
but I could not eat a one
for God was in that orange.
I could not touch what did not belong to me.
The priest came,
he said God was even in Hitler.
I did not believe him
for if God were in Hitler
then God would be in me.
I did not hear the bird sounds.
They had left.
I did not see the speechless clouds,
I saw only the little white dish of my faith
breaking in the crater.
I kept saying:
I've got to have something to hold on to.
People gave me Bibles, crucifixes,
a yellow daisy,
but I could not touch them,
I who was a house full of bowel movement,

I who was a defaced altar,
I who wanted to crawl toward God
could not move or eat bread.

So I ate myself,
bite by bite,
and the tears washed me,
wave after cowardly wave,
swallowing canker after canker
and Jesus stood over me looking down
and He laughed to find me gone,
and put His mouth to mine
and gave me His air.

My kindred, my brother, I said
and gave the yellow daisy
to the crazy woman in the next bed.

This shocking poem is taken from Sexton's collection *The Awful Rowing Toward God*, which was published posthumously. She had been looking over its proofs on the day she took her own life.

Sexton struggles with both her faith and her depression in the poem, the two struggles combining with such pain and fury that we the reader can feel as overwhelmed as Sexton herself. It is not clear whether Sexton's depression has led to her lack of faith, or her lack of faith has led to her depression. The first verse is full of unflinching metaphors about Sexton herself as she loses her belief in God. She is rendered inhuman and unlovely, first as stone and then as a side of mutton (this image contrasts with Jesus being the Lamb of God). In another disordered image at the end of the second verse, she is 'a house full of bowel movement'.

The second verse paints a picture of her lying in bed, presumably in a psychiatric hospital (there is a 'crazy woman' in the next bed). Visitors come: one brings oranges, another is a priest. But they cannot reach her. Nor is she conscious of the bird sounds, or the 'speechless clouds'. All she can focus on is her loss of faith – that faith imagined as tiny as a 'little white' dish, brought to dramatic life as she imagines it 'breaking'. Nothing helps her loss of faith or fulfils her need to have 'something to hold on to', literally and metaphorically – a natural response to that feeling of falling so well evoked by Gerard Manley Hopkins in the poem earlier. (I remember clinging on to my husband or my mother when I was unwell for what seemed like life itself.)

In the last verse, Jesus does appear. He laughs to find her gone from Him. Yet, in a final key gesture, Sexton receives the kiss of life from Jesus. She greets Jesus as her brother, and hands on the symbolic yellow daisy. This final hint of hope makes the poem more bearable and suggests that faith can help after all. I was brought up a Catholic and my faith has sustained me over the years, though not without many struggles. I am conscious that many others, like Sexton, have an even more difficult relationship with religious belief if they have one at all.

11. 'Who Ne'er his Bread in Sorrow Ate' by Johann Wolfgang von Goethe, translated by Henry Wadsworth Longfellow

Who ne'er his bread in sorrow ate,
Who ne'er the mournful midnight hours
Weeping upon his bed has sate,
He knows you not, ye Heavenly Powers.

So much is being argued in a mere four compact lines, putting forward an overarching philosophy of life with exceptional efficiency. Goethe's point is that only through experiencing the extreme pain of worldly human misery are we able to meet and engage with the higher 'Heavenly Powers' of a more spiritual grace.

Rather than the more usual 'God', these powers sound impersonal, as if they were the laws of physics explaining everything; and we will only be fully human and wise if we engage with them. The need to know and meet these powers in turn makes sense of human sorrow and suffering. Such periods of anguish are necessary and beneficial even as they allow us to access this spirit of grace. No experience, however dark, is without value, a concept that provides me with solace.

Goethe's argument is more powerful thanks to the evocative way he conjures up our sorrowful plight. His image of suffering is domestic and personal: we can picture someone sadly eating alone, that word 'bread' evoking a household scene; and imagine that person crying in bed. These images contrast with the more impersonal 'Heavenly Powers', their importance emphasised by Goethe's use of capital letters. Ultimately, our suffering is worth it for the prize of this spiritual connection with something superior.

These four lines are an extract from the novel *Wilhelm Meister's Apprenticeship*. The protagonist finds an old man playing his harp, singing in 'low broken tones' the verse reproduced above. Music brings an extra charge to poetry: many poems, after all, were originally sung or recited aloud in pre-literate times. Wilhelm stands by the door to listen. The lament of the old harpist, the power of the music and the words he sings, reach deep into the heart of Wilhelm, who is moved to tears, and who finds himself able, at last, to release the 'pains that pressed upon his soul'. By allowing our feelings, we can discharge them in a cathartic way.

12.   'Dog in the Valley' by Tishani Doshi

Last night
I heard a dog
in the valley
puncturing the hills
with a sound
from a long
time ago.
It was the sound
of a man and woman
falling out of love,
the sound of a century
caught in the dark –
barking, barking.
A deep-throated howl
made under stars,
made against death,
insisting there are drums
underground,
cymbals in the cloud,
a music that goes on and on
because someone
somewhere
is listening.

This poem immediately takes us to a seemingly barren or empty place. We are rooted in a specific location, in a specific time by a specific sound – what sounds like the simple barking of a dog. The poem can feel quite hard to parse at first. The reader, like the speaker, is deliberately left alone in the dark in the first few lines. This feeling of not knowing what is going on is amplified by the poet's use of short lines, which for a moment almost threaten to peter out with 'from a long / time ago': they feel like the echoes made by something small in a large, silent space.

Yet the poem's mood changes with the certainty evoked by the unequivocal 'It was the sound…'. We go, quickly, from not knowing, to being shocked. The key surprise is that what we think is the sound of a dog barking becomes the sound of an emotion: the sound of a failed relationship, remembered as having an almost historic, universal reach that speaks to a whole era. Now the poem reveals a new scale and ambition.

The bleakness of the poem's opening gives way slowly to a more optimistic vision. The 'deep-throated howl / made under stars, / made against death' gives a sense of hope emerging from the darkness of love gone wrong and a 'century / caught in the dark'. Nature, deeply personal emotions, and the rest of the world seem entangled together in a cosmic, cathartic din. Cymbals and drums are placed within the clouds and the earth, and sound with defiance.

The 'music that goes on and on' is not something ethereal and separate from us. Night turns out not to be a void where sounds get lost, but a place where sounds are heard with us bearing witness to them. In the last few lines, intimacy asserts itself after all the dramas. Quietly, someone, somewhere, is listening. In turn, even though we are the ones reading the poem, it is as if the poem itself is listening to us. A connection is made. It may be all we need.

13. 'Ode on Melancholy' by John Keats

No, no, go not to Lethe, neither twist
   Wolf's-bane, tight-rooted, for its poisonous wine;
Nor suffer thy pale forehead to be kiss'd
   By nightshade, ruby grape of Proserpine;
     Make not your rosary of yew-berries,
   Nor let the beetle, nor the death-moth be
     Your mournful Psyche, nor the downy owl
A partner in your sorrow's mysteries;
   For shade to shade will come too drowsily,
     And drown the wakeful anguish of the soul.

But when the melancholy fit shall fall
   Sudden from heaven like a weeping cloud,
That fosters the droop-headed flowers all,
   And hides the green hill in an April shroud;
Then glut thy sorrow on a morning rose,
   Or on the rainbow of the salt sand-wave,
     Or on the wealth of globed peonies;
Or if thy mistress some rich anger shows,
   Emprison her soft hand, and let her rave,
     And feed deep, deep upon her peerless eyes.

She dwells with Beauty—Beauty that must die;
   And Joy, whose hand is ever at his lips
Bidding adieu; and aching Pleasure nigh,
   Turning to poison while the bee-mouth sips:
Ay, in the very temple of Delight
   Veil'd Melancholy has her sovran shrine,

Though seen of none save him whose strenuous tongue
   Can burst Joy's grape against his palate fine;
His soul shalt taste the sadness of her might,
    And be among her cloudy trophies hung.

Here Keats turns melancholy into something beautiful and inevitable that we do well to accept. Partly he succeeds in persuading us because of the force of his argument; partly it is because of the power of his images and dreamy invocations, which overwhelm any resistance with their sensual magic. First, the argument. He develops an apparent paradox: that pleasure and pain are intimately connected, and that sadness rests at the core of joy. He addresses us directly, building his argument, stanza by stanza, till by the end of the third verse we too can accept rather than be defeated by melancholy.

The first verse tells the reader what not to do, using 'no', 'not' and 'nor' in quick succession to drive home his point that one should not try to escape sadness, be it mental stupor (the River Lethe is the river of oblivion in Greek mythology); or by physical destruction through suicide (wolf's-bane plants are poisonous); by brushing with the poisonous nightshade plant, or by drinking wine from the mythical Queen of the Underworld (Proserpine). Here Keats deploys his second weapon in convincing us of his argument: his use of striking imagery, in the making of a rosary with yew berries (also poisonous), suggesting prayers for the dying. Equally, we should not become obsessed with the symbols of death and misery: the beetle, the death-moth and the owl. All of this will make the anguish of the soul drowsy. Instead, we should remain alert to suffering.

The second stanza tells us what we should do instead when afflicted with melancholy. We must engage fully in nature's beauty in order to overcome sorrow. When melancholy strikes, like a sudden thunderstorm that makes the sky weep, we should feed our pain by gazing upon a rose that blossoms only in the morning, or the rainbows over the sea, or the bounteous peony flowers, all described with such lavish deliciousness and sensuality that we melt with the force of his argument.

The third verse explains the injunctions of the second. We should glut ourselves on nature's beauty, he argues, because sadness and joy are deeply intertwined: the shrine of melancholy is inside the 'temple of Delight'. Now Beauty, Joy and Pleasure are all personified and are all suspect. Beauty must die, Joy must say goodbye, while Pleasure turns toxic. Sadness is the price we pay for happiness, and the person who, in the wonderfully sensual image, 'can burst Joy's grape against his palate fine' is, Keats suggests, often the most susceptible to Melancholy. There's some consolation in that.

There's consolation too in the way the poem requires us to concentrate, and in doing so distracts us from our worries. Bursting with allusions and arguments, this ode is particularly good at rooting us in the moment: it requires careful unpicking, and therefore absorbs us entirely for a period of time. Finally, there's consolation to be had in the poem's languid pace. Each stanza is one long, drawn-out sentence, a slow-moving pace that is underlined by the predictable rhyme scheme and measured rhythm of the ode form. The poem has a soothing and hynoptic, musical quality, the euphony of its words caressing our jangled spirits: the 'downy owl' and 'globed peonies'. Meanwhile, 'wakeful anguish' is the perfect description of insomnia.

Ultimately, the poem's message is that sadness is part of every pleasure because nothing lasts, a point of great personal relevance to Keats, who died young, as had his mother and brother. Fleeting pleasures may entail grief, but perhaps should be enjoyed all the more for that.

SPRING

Time for Hope

Introduction to Spring

With Spring comes new hope, and here are writers to guide you through a period of renewal. You can win through. That is the message of the first couple of poems in this section. You have the power within you to change things. If this does not feel true to you right now, reading these words may help.

Bashō begins with a promise that we too are part of nature and our human music never stops. Dickinson adds, you need strength and hope. These are weapons already in your arsenal, waiting only for you to deploy them.

Once through the bleakness, there needs to come a period of introspective healing: self-forgiveness, self-love, and self-restoration. These next few poems acknowledge that ability of the human psyche to embrace hope and kindness just as much as despair – and that all things are fleeting, and we need not be resistant to change. Herbert reassures us that healing, reparation and compassion are all possible, even when we feel 'guilty of dust and sin'. The kindly voice of love in response to the injured speaker in Herbert's dialogue brings together the two halves of the self. The invitation to forgive oneself is followed by Mary Oliver's message of self-acceptance; we must relax, and 'let the soft animal of your body / love what it loves'. We have a place in the family of things. Mackay's song is about the power of tears. Releasing our pain and sorrow paves the way for recovery and growth: it lets the joy come in. Pitter and Coolidge seek inspiration in the opportunity of this bright, new dawn. In Coolidge's words, we can 'take heart with the day, and begin again'.

The last few pieces in this section are there to help you keep going, to ride the storm until it ends, as Hammerstein puts it. Many of the passages here, such as Milton's lines from 'Paradise Lost', are about re-establishing a sense of agency and empowerment. Needham invites us to find our fortitude. Gaskell urges us to act. Spring comes with a defiant rejection of sadness and a strong rebuilding of inner strength.

14. 'The Temple Bell Stops' by Matsuo Bashō, translated by Robert Bly

The temple bell stops –
But the sound keeps coming
out of the flowers

It is the combination of the two different, indeed seemingly unrelated, images of the temple bell and the flower that surprise us here in Bashō's haiku.

Some small facet of the natural world explodes into new existence under the poet's scrutiny. Here it is the striking image of flowers, which we imagine to be silent, harnessing and connecting to the previous ringing of a bell, presumably by a monk. The 'sound' emanates from the flowers even if we might expect the poet to say 'scent'. The effect is of the flowers' fragrance acquiring a new amplitude that takes it beyond the five senses, or links them all synesthetically in a deepened appreciation of nature.

Human endeavours (like the ringing of a bell) and lives seem finite, but in fact are connected to the infinity of the natural world. The dash at the end of the first line evokes the dying out of the sound of the bell, leaving a silence within the poem that is even deeper than that suggested by a line break. But that same sound is picked up in nature, through the agency of the flower. We too are part of nature and our human music never stops.

So much philosophy and feeling are packed into three short lines. Which makes this an easy poem to learn, as indeed are all haikus. (Haiku is the name given to this sort of traditional Japanese nature poem of seventeen syllables, typically in three lines of five, seven and five – though not all haikus, including this one, follow this exact syllabic form: here the second line has only six syllables.) It is a poem that I turn to whenever I feel a pang of grief at the memory of my late mother, who died nearly three years ago. Her temple bell has stopped. But her spirit keeps coming.

15.   '"Hope" is the thing with feathers' by Emily Dickinson

'Hope' is the thing with feathers –
That perches in the soul –
And sings the tune without the words –
And never stops – at all –

And sweetest – in the Gale – is heard –
And sore must be the storm –
That could abash the little Bird
That kept so many warm –

I've heard it in the chillest land –
And on the strangest Sea –
Yet – never – in Extremity,
It asked a crumb – of me.

Dickinson gradually allows the analogy between hope and a little bird to unfold: the bird itself only appears directly at the end of the second stanza. She thereby avoids a commonplace simile that hope equals a singing bird, instead giving us time to think about both birds and hope in new ways.

Her strange 'thing with feathers' lives inside us, as if our ribs were like a branch; and unlike every other bird, it never stops singing. Her idiosyncratic use of capital letters for certain words, personalising them, helps to draw our attention to them. Meanwhile all the dashes force us to pause. They could represent the obstacles the little bird has to hop over: in the line about the gale, there are three dashes, suggesting this is a particularly large obstacle, as if the bird is being beaten back by the wind. The rhyme scheme, unpronounced at first, strengthens as it goes, culminating in a triple rhyme in the final three lines, which affirm the poem's message that hope can weather any storm. This certainty is confirmed by the poem's final and only full stop.

In stages, we recognise the obstacles that 'hope' steadily over-comes, with the last verse emerging as the most personal. Believing in this kind of hope – never-ending, inside us, asking nothing of us in return – is essential. I especially like the way that hope is part of us. It is not something we need to find or earn by our good behaviour. There is nothing transactional about it. It is there, inside us, anyway.

Dickinson's own life reaffirms this: a story of absolute hope. She produced over 1,800 poems. Yet only a few (heavily edited and rewritten) were published while she was alive. A good message, and a good poem, to share with any aspiring writer or indeed any creative artist.

16. 'Love' by George Herbert

Love bade me welcome; yet my soul drew back,
*   Guilty of dust and sin.*
But quick-eyed Love, observing me grow slack
*   From my first entrance in,*
Drew nearer to me, sweetly questioning,
*   If I lacked any thing.*

A guest, I answered, worthy to be here:
*   Love said, You shall be he.*
I, the unkind, ungrateful? Ah, my dear,
*   I cannot look on thee.*
Love took my hand, and smiling did reply,
*   'Who made the eyes but I?'*

Truth Lord, but I have marred them: let my shame
*   Go where it doth deserve.*
And know you not, says Love, who bore the blame?
*   My dear, then I will serve.*
You must sit down, says Love, and taste my meat.
*   So I did sit and eat.*

Here is a conversation between two states of mind, both of which can exist within one consciousness. The alternating indents are confirmation of a dialogue between the narrator, who feels unworthy, and Love, who is personified: Herbert is using Love rather than God.

The voice of Love is enthusiastic and eager in the first verse: witness the short and easy-to-voice syllables in 'Love bade me welcome'. By contrast, the narrator's voice is slow and heavy, matched by the heavy syllables that take longer to pronounce in 'my soul drew back' and 'guilty of dust and sin' (I can't imagine a better description of feeling depressed); similarly, with 'quick-eyed Love' and 'grow slack'. Love is warm and friendly, someone who draws nearer, questions sweetly – not someone who judges us, as we sometimes imagine God is doing.

In the second verse, the narrator still feels unworthy of being Love's guest. Love asks: 'Who made the eyes but I?' Throughout, Love is questioning our answers, rather than answering our questions. Yet the narrator is lovable: he was created by Love in the first place, witness the word play on 'eyes', meaning both the eyes through which we see and I as in a person.

By the final verse, all doubt is gone. Herbert unites heart and soul and the self. Faith is restored to the narrator. Bread is accepted (the food is metaphorical, representing the Christian sacrament of Communion). The narrator has felt shame, rather than guilt. He hasn't just done something wrong. He *is* something wrong. But through the gentle invitation of Love, he finally lets himself be loved for who he is. He accepts Love's reasoning, that he is good enough to join in, eating the food set before him. He does so with ease and simplicity, suggested by the six single syllables of the last line. The master becomes the servant.

Love gets the last word in the poem. Love is not something we trade, or exchange. We cannot earn it, nor destroy it. It is something we are, in a similar way that Dickinson suggested that hope is also part of our fabric. This is a poem for anyone who doubts their lovability, which probably means all of us, at least from time to time, and certainly includes me. I recite and re-recite this poem, especially if I am lying awake at night, because it is one of the few poems I know by heart. When I do, I feel a weight fall from my shoulders. The relief is palpable. It doesn't matter if I'm unkind and ungrateful (and I often feel I am). It is irrelevant if I feel shameful in some way. It turns out I do not need to be worthy of love. It is something I am. And so are you.

17.   'Wild Geese' by Mary Oliver

You do not have to be good.
You do not have to walk on your knees
for a hundred miles through the desert, repenting.
You only have to let the soft animal of your body
love what it loves.
Tell me about despair, yours, and I will tell you mine.
Meanwhile the world goes on.
Meanwhile the sun and the clear pebbles of the rain
are moving across the landscapes,
over the prairies and the deep trees,
the mountains and the rivers.
Meanwhile the wild geese, high in the clean blue air,
are heading home again.
Whoever you are, no matter how lonely,
the world offers itself to your imagination,
calls to you like the wild geese, harsh and exciting –
over and over announcing your place
in the family of things.

As if in the middle of an intimate conversation between the poet and reader, the poem begins with what seems strange advice. Oliver urges us to unlearn one of the first lessons we are taught – to be good. In fact, we do not have to be good to be loved. Instead, all we need to do is reconnect with our essential loving, animal nature. All we must do is to 'let' this happen.

The intimacy between poet and reader is further heightened in Oliver's promise that from now on we will trust each other sufficiently to open up, as we are equal in our humanity and our despair. 'Tell me about despair, yours, and I will tell you mine' shows how fiercely the poet wants to connect with her reader: this is the heart of the poem's power – we are loving creatures, says Oliver.

We can mirror nature's own sense of being unperturbed. (Note the 'clear pebbles' of rain: an arresting image given the solidity of stone compared to the translucence of water.) The natural world unfolds anyway, not because it has been told it must or should. This sense of freedom is conjured in the metaphor of the wild geese of the poem's title. We too can fly free; we too can be kindred spirits to each other, calling to each other, just as the geese do. We are a part of something bigger, an affinity that nonetheless acknowledges mutual pain suggested in the word 'harsh'. Oliver's message is powerful for not being sentimental: we too can head home, back into nature, both in our lifetimes and perhaps after our deaths.

Our place in 'the family of things' may even be our final home, just as the geese are perhaps heading home to their last resting place. I often find myself imagining the spirit of my late mother as a bird, finally flying free after the horrors of cancer and chemotherapy. She might even be one of Oliver's wild geese, 'high in the clean blue air', her place assured in the family of things.

That feeling of belonging is what the poem leaves us with. For some periods of my life, I have felt as if I had no place in the world, as if I was unworthy, a sentiment with which many may identify. But Oliver's world is one in which we all belong; one where we all have a place, no matter how lowly or useless we feel ourselves to be; and one, finally, in which we do not have to be other than who we are. It doesn't get better, really.

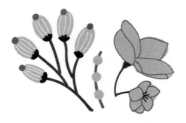

18.　'O Ye Tears!' by Charles Mackay

O ye tears! O ye tears! that have long refused to flow,
Ye are welcome to my heart, thawing, thawing, like the snow;
I feel, the hard clod soften, and the early snow-drops spring,
And the healing fountains gush, and the wildernesses sing.

O ye tears! O ye tears! I am thankful that ye run;
Though ye trickle in the darkness, ye shall glisten in the sun.
The rainbow cannot shine, if the drops refuse to fall,
And the eyes that cannot weep, are the saddest eyes of all.

O ye tears! O ye tears! till I felt ye on my cheek,
I was selfish in my sorrow; I was stubborn, I was weak.
Ye, have giv'n me strength to conquer, and I stand erect and free,
And know that I am human, by the light of sympathy.

O ye tears! O ye tears! ye relieve me of my pain;
The barren rock of Pride has been stricken once again:
Like the rock that Moses smote amid Horeb's burning sand,
It yields the flowing water, to make gladness in the land.

There is light upon my path! there is sunshine in my heart!
And the leaf and fruit of life shall not utterly depart.
Ye restore to me the freshness and the bloom of long ago –
O ye tears! happy tears! I am thankful that ye flow!

Mackay finds strength and renewal in his tears; they help the healing process. There is something moving about a buttoned-up man allowing himself to show his emotions. Even now, many of us struggle to reveal our vulnerability, imagining it a weakness, rather than something that is part of our common humanity.

He had been 'stubborn' in his sorrow, too proud to feel pity for himself, to let himself mourn. The landscape inside him was frozen, bleak, unable to grow. He refers to the barren rocks of his pride, akin to the rock that Moses strikes 'amid Horeb's burning sand'. (Horeb is another name for Mount Sinai, where Moses received the Ten Commandments.)

Throughout the poem, the poet turns to nature to convey his emotional state. His heart was frozen but, thanks to his newfound ability to cry, now it is thawing like snow in Winter. Equally, the hard 'clods' of his unexpressed feelings are beginning to soften, just as frozen lumps of earth are loosened and broken up as the weather warms. He identifies his own healing with that to be found in gushing fountains and wildernesses that sing.

Nature also provides a metaphor to explain the complexity of the nuanced mingling of sadness with joy: the rainbow. The two are inextricably linked in real life. Without drops of rainwater to reflect the light, a rainbow could not exist.

At last, expressing his feelings and allowing himself to cry renews him, just as nature constantly renews itself. He feels youthful again, restored to 'the freshness and the bloom of long ago'. By letting out his pain, he finds himself able to let in joy. Nature has been his companion every step of the way. This poem can be your companion if you are finding it hard to express sadness. My thanks to Mackay and his invitation to allow our grief, and indeed all our feelings: to let our hearts thaw like snow.

19. 'For Sleep, or Death' by Ruth Pitter

Cure me with quietness,
Bless me with peace;
Comfort my heaviness,
Stay me with ease.
Stillness in solitude
Send down like dew;
Mine armour of fortitude
Piece and make new:
That when I rise again
I may shine bright
As the sky after rain,
Day after night.

Is Pitter soliciting courage before she dies in a deathbed sigh? Is the reference to 'when I rise again' about ascending into heaven? Or is this simply a nightly prayer about trying to get to sleep, and praying for peace and calm, followed by morning renewal? Pitter does not resolve this haunting ambiguity found in the poem's title.

Her use of the imperative at the start of most lines, pleading for comfort and inner strength, adds to the poem's gravitas. Yet there is a paradox between the solemnity of the message and the way the words flow with such ease and simplicity. The rhythm provides a certain comfort: short words and a regular pattern of a six-syllable line, followed by a four-syllable.

What Pitter does establish is the way our moods can find their parallel in nature. She invites God, or some higher power, to gift her the quietness, peace and stillness she seeks, as if he was sending them 'down like dew' from the heavens.

This parallel carries through to the last four lines: she hopes she may take on the characteristics of the 'sky after rain' and borrow from nature's own ability to renew itself each morning. Which is something I find attractive: the idea that psychological growth is ongoing. We are constantly learning and growing. Every morning we may have to start again. Our 'armour of fortitude' must be continually remade to fit, to 'piece and make new'.

This is not something to be feared. It is part of who we are, just as nature is constantly renewing and reinventing itself. Which is also the reason I dislike asking children what they want to be when they grow up (to borrow a line from Michelle Obama). We are always becoming who we are meant to be.

20. 'New Every Morning' by Susan Coolidge

Every morn is the world made new.
You who are weary of sorrow and sinning,
Here is a beautiful hope for you, –
A hope for me and a hope for you.

All the past things are past and over;
The tasks are done and the tears are shed.
Yesterday's errors let yesterday cover;
Yesterday's wounds, which smarted and bled,
Are healed with the healing which night has shed.

Yesterday now is a part of forever,
Bound up in a sheaf, which God holds tight,
With glad days, and sad days, and bad days, which never
Shall visit us more with their bloom and their blight,
Their fullness of sunshine or sorrowful night.

Let them go, since we cannot re-live them,
Cannot undo and cannot atone;
God in his mercy receive, forgive them!
Only the new days are our own;
To-day is ours, and to-day alone.

Here are the skies all burnished brightly,
Here is the spent earth all re-born,
Here are the tired limbs springing lightly
To face the sun and to share with the morn
In the chrism of dew and the cool of dawn.

Every day is a fresh beginning;
Listen, my soul, to the glad refrain,
And, spite of old sorrow and older sinning,
And puzzles forecasted and possible pain,
Take heart with the day, and begin again.

Coolidge, like Pitter, focuses on how we are renewed each morning, and how every day is a fresh beginning. But how many of us live our lives with this comforting thought in mind? As Coolidge herself understands, many of us struggle to embrace this truth. We imagine we are defined by mistakes we have made in the past. That reinvention is impossible. That we cannot change. That we are doomed to repeat ourselves.

Her poem is a passionate call to arms: instead of dwelling on our past mistakes, we should embrace a spring-clean for the soul. The poem's regular and controlled rhyme scheme is persuasive, giving her wisdom a reassuring consistency. Yesterday is gone, and there is no point revisiting what has passed, whether sad or happy.

Coolidge's use of repetition helps to drum her points home. Take the fifth verse where the first three lines begin with 'Here': she grabs our attention, to take us beyond our theoretical knowledge that every day is a new beginning and make this happen. That way, we will draw strength from the natural world's daily renewal, and become burnished like the sky, re-born like the spent earth, and find our tired limbs 'springing lightly' as if we were gambolling spring lambs.

Coolidge's philosophy and compassion may have been influenced by personal experience. She began writing after the end of the vicious American Civil War, when she had worked as a nurse. Her views hint at someone who had interacted with death daily, for example in her reference to 'Yesterday's wounds, which smarted and bled' in the second verse: something she knew all about and which gives the poem something of its urgency to embrace living, fully, in the present moment.

That philosophy reflects the practice of mindfulness, which has helped many improve their wellbeing, including me. Rather than regretting the past or worrying about the future, I try to embrace the now, with feeling. Which is why I love the fact that Coolidge asks us to 'Take *heart* with the day, and begin again' (my italics). Mindfulness for me is about living, right here, right now, fully in our hearts, rather than just our heads – a good philosophy with which to start the day. And we can always begin again – whatever time, and however grim our day has been up to that point.

21. From 'Paradise Lost' by John Milton

The mind is its own place, and in itself
Can make a Heaven of Hell, a Hell of Heaven.

In these two lines, about our ability to create our own reality, the speaker is Lucifer, or Satan, also called 'The lost Archangel' by Milton. He has just fallen from Heaven to the newly made Hell and is adjusting to this new place in which he finds himself. And he is persuading himself that his mind is not going to change just because he finds himself living in a pit of fire and brimstone. Hell can be as good as Heaven any day, he boasts, even if celestial light is not in evidence. Hell is a mental state, not a place. The truth is not out there; it is in here, in the mind.

The context in which Milton was writing was a religious one, and he would have been unlikely to have agreed with Lucifer. But the way he reverses the narrative of mental suffering by giving us some agency over our thoughts is relevant whether we believe in God or not. The imaginative power of our minds is acknowledged. We perceive reality not as it is, but as we are. It follows that in any given situation, it is less about the circumstances in which we find ourselves, and more how we respond to our circumstances. And that is within our power.

This is such an encouraging thought, one to bear in mind whenever we feel helpless and impotent in the face of despair. I remember losing any sense of my own agency when I was depressed. It seemed as if my only hope was to rely on others, whether they were doctors, psychiatrists, therapists or psychologists. And of course, their support was crucial. But part of my recovery has been to realise that I have a part to play too. I can make a difference. I can change my thoughts and feelings and use my imagination to write a more positive, and more joyful story. As Milton puts it so beautifully, I can create my own Heaven out of Hell.

22. 'You'll Never Walk Alone' by Oscar Hammerstein II

When you walk through a storm,
Hold your head up high
And don't be afraid of the dark;

At the end of the storm
There's a golden sky
And the sweet, silver song of the lark.

Walk on through the wind,
Walk on through the rain,
Though your dreams be tossed and blown;

Walk on, walk on with hope in your heart
And you'll never walk alone,
You'll never walk alone;

Walk on, walk on with hope in your heart
And you'll never walk alone,
You'll never walk alone.

One reason this song has resonated over the years in so many different contexts is the simplicity and effectiveness of its central metaphor: a storm is equivalent to life's troubles. What is true of storms is true of life. They end: an ending here rendered with tenderness thanks to the image of a golden sky, enlivened by lark song, which contrasts with the storm's darkness.

Another reason for the poem's power is the sheer chutzpah and determination of the narrator, willing us on. Repetition of the need to keep walking in the second verse stiffens our resolve, as does the reward we are promised. If we press on, we will never walk alone. This is what we want to believe when facing our own storm: that others will join forces with us. The hope within us will be matched by the hope within others. Read these words, and we will believe this to be true.

The song has served as a moving tribute ever since it was first written by Hammerstein and his musical partner Richard Rodgers for the 1945 musical *Carousel*. It is sung twice: first, to comfort a woman following the death of her husband, and second, at her daughter's graduation ceremony. It became the anthem for Liverpool Football Club in the early 1960s and took on new symbolism as a moving tribute to those killed in the Hillsborough disaster of April 1989. More recently it became Britain's most listened to song of 2020 during the Covid-19 pandemic, and its text was to be found pinned up on the walls of NHS wards around the country. I chose it as the title for this anthology as poetry is my companion – as you will know by now. Given the poem's popularity, lots of other people think the same way too.

23. 'A Blessing' by James Wright

Just off the highway to Rochester, Minnesota,
Twilight bounds softly forth on the grass.
And the eyes of those two Indian ponies
Darken with kindness.
They have come gladly out of the willows
To welcome my friend and me.
We step over the barbed wire into the pasture
Where they have been grazing all day, alone.
They ripple tensely, they can hardly contain their happiness
That we have come.
They bow shyly as wet swans. They love each other.
There is no loneliness like theirs.
At home once more,
They begin munching the young tufts of spring in the darkness.
I would like to hold the slenderer one in my arms,
For she has walked over to me
And nuzzled my left hand.
She is black and white,
Her mane falls wild on her forehead,
And the light breeze moves me to caress her long ear
That is delicate as the skin over a girl's wrist.
Suddenly I realize
That if I stepped out of my body I would break
Into blossom.

As we leave the highway, Twilight, personified, bounds forth like a pony, soft to the touch, landing on the grass. Wright blurs the boundaries between us and the animal world as the ponies take on human characteristics – their eyes 'darken with kindness'; they feel human emotions: they can 'hardly contain their happiness'; and they themselves seem to merge with birds when they bow as shyly as swans.

The narrator falls for one of the ponies almost as if it were human, a point made explicit when he describes the pony's ear as soft as a girl's wrist. Traces of the ugliness of the man-made world – the highway, the barbed wire – have been forgotten in the joy of this transcendent merging of identities.

The poem's line breaks allow the narrator to slowly reveal his unfolding awakening. Initially, the story is about 'we' and 'they'. Then the poem becomes more personal with the use of 'I'. Only in the final lines does the poet realise the big thing that this homely encounter has taught him, a suddenness intensified by the alliteration of 'body', 'blossom' and 'break', and the continuation of the meaning of the line after the word 'break' or enjambment: he almost leaps to his conclusion. He can escape his materiality and loneliness: his use of the matter-of-fact 'stepped' makes the transcendence he describes as simple as putting one foot in front of another.

What happened in the pasture is hard to put into words. The poet gives us the surreal metaphor of his breaking 'into blossom' to describe his need to transcend his physical limits. He feels something extraordinary and has found a way to share that feeling.

His words come back to me whenever I chance upon horses. Wright intensifies my experience, as if a small glow inside me that has been doused down roars back to life. A simple visit to a field, and a pony nuzzling my hand, becomes something far more powerful.

24. From *The Black Riders* by Violet Needham

The password is fortitude.

There's something powerful about an all-embracing philosophy of life being packed into four brief words: that fortitude, or strength in the face of adversity (the word comes from the Latin 'fortis' meaning strong), is the answer to all of life's challenges. Find this courage, and you have been given the key to dealing with whatever may trouble you. Just one password solves everything: a view stunning in its simplicity, which is what gives this sentence its punch and us an answer to our uncertainties.

It is a password which acknowledges that life is painful. We need strength precisely because we will all experience challenges. The more we accept that no-one escapes from painful feelings, the easier it will be to cope with them when they inevitably arise. What we resist, persists, as I said in my introduction. I think that's one reason my mother introduced us to this saying early on in our lives. She was preparing us children for the road, rather than trying to smooth the road for the child. And she knew we would need fortitude en route.

'The password is fortitude' was one of her favourite responses to any setback, one she shared not just with us but in turn with her grandchildren. When one child was having a tricky time at university, she sent him a postcard with Needham's words, telling him to stick it or them on his bathroom mirror: he still has the postcard, a treasured memento of his granny and her philosophy of life now she has died. Thus, for me at least, the phrase is drenched with a feeling of family solidarity and support across the generations, and the echo of my mother's voice. When she herself was courageously facing her own cancer towards the end of her life, she again found comfort in Needham's words. I hope I will inherit at least some of her fortitude.

The quotation comes from a book called *The Black Riders*, which was Needham's first novel, published in 1939 when she was sixty-three years old (encouraging for late starters). It was the first of what became a highly popular series of children's books about the orphaned Dick Fauconbois and his adventures as part of a rebel movement in an oppressed European state. We read the book as children; I encouraged my own children to do the same. A shared experience, and one which gave our family a password for how to try to live our lives.

25.   'The Unknown Bird' by Edward Thomas

Three lovely notes he whistled, too soft to be heard
If others sang; but others never sang
In the great beech-wood all that May and June.
No one saw him: I alone could hear him
Though many listened. Was it but four years
Ago? or five? He never came again.

Oftenest when I heard him I was alone,
Nor could I ever make another hear.
La-la-la! he called, seeming far-off –
As if a cock crowed past the edge of the world,
As if the bird or I were in a dream.
Yet that he travelled through the trees and sometimes
Neared me, was plain, though somehow distant still
He sounded. All the proof is – I told men
What I had heard.

I never knew a voice,
Man, beast, or bird, better than this. I told
The naturalists; but neither had they heard
Anything like the notes that did so haunt me,
I had them clear by heart and have them still.
Four years, or five, have made no difference. Then
As now that La-la-la! was bodiless sweet:
Sad more than joyful it was, if I must say
That it was one or other, but if sad
'Twas sad only with joy too, too far off
For me to taste it. But I cannot tell

If truly never anything but fair
The days were when he sang, as now they seem.
This surely I know, that I who listened then,
Happy sometimes, sometimes suffering
A heavy body and a heavy heart,
Now straightway, if I think of it, become
Light as that bird wandering beyond my shore.

An unknown bird whistles just three notes, the 'bodiless sweet' la-la-la. A mystery: only Thomas hears the birdsong, 'though many listened'. No naturalists recognise the notes he describes. This one bird alone sang that late Spring, the entire May and on into June. Might it have all been a dream? The ambiguity leaves us intrigued and hungry to discover the answer, but the obscurities continue through the poem and keep us guessing. The bird is sometimes in plain sight, though somehow distant too. The birdsong is more 'sad than joyful', but it is an uncertain sadness, as it also contains joy.

Thomas contrasts this elusiveness of the experience he is trying to capture with his own more straightforward reality as the poem's narrator. The solidity of his reactions makes his story more believable. He is convinced he has never heard a better 'voice'. He has discussed what happened with others; he can remember the notes he heard clearly, over several years.

Above all, he is certain about the powerful effect the memory has on him, encapsulated in the last two lines. This memory creates such lightness in Thomas that it counterbalances all other moods, and he becomes as carefree as the bird itself. However happy or otherwise Thomas's life was when he first heard that la-la-la, now when he thinks back to that time, he experiences nothing but a sense of exhilaration.

We are left hopeful that we too might hear our own mysterious and metaphorical bird, and experience a similar, all-encompassing euphoria. Moments of extreme exhilaration can indeed be odd, as are the circumstances in which they arise. They may be prompted in our own lives by something as equally inexplicable as Thomas's mystical encounter with an unknown bird.

26. From *North and South* by Elizabeth Gaskell

Thinking has, many a time, made me sad, darling; but doing never did in all my life. My theory is a sort of parody on the maxim of 'Get money, my son, honestly if you can; but get money.' My precept is, 'Do something, my sister, do good if you can; but, at any rate, do something.'

These words come from Gaskell's novel *North and South*, written at a time of great inequality and hardship in the North, arguably because a new breed of industrialist was pursuing financial success and money above all else. Here Gaskell comes up with an alternative to the get-rich narrative of her time in favour of a new maxim about what makes us happy. Her answer is that we should do, rather than think.

She contrasts her own maxim with the prevailing advice of the time, parodied here in a colloquial, avuncular voice: the use of the familiar 'my son', with the suggestion that the advice is reasonable and balanced ('honestly if you can'). But it is ruthless and corrupt: get rich, even by dishonest means. Gaskell's own guidance echoes the rhythm and syntax of this earlier maxim, and has a similar chatty feel, but swaps its brutality for something wise and gentle that speaks to our human frailty.

Her advice appeals, as her voice is not preachy or holier-than-thou. She understands that the additional pressure to do something good may be beyond us and softens her tone with the mitigation 'if you can', acknowledging that we may not be able to pull off something of benefit to others. Yes, we might do good, but that is optional. We feel understood in our powerlessness to necessarily produce results and can relate to what Gaskell advises. Any action at all will benefit us if we are stuck in our thoughts, as is so often the case when we are depressed or anxious.

Her conviction is the fruit of long experience ('in all my life') and wins us over. I've found Gaskell's maxim never lets me down when my thoughts go round and round. Doing something is the answer, be that sharpening pencils, or sweeping the floor, or making a cake. It is advice I share with my (at times) introspective teenage children. Gaskell's words make all of us feel more purposeful. Sometimes we end up doing something together. And, sometimes, we even do good.

SUMMER

Time for Joy

Introduction to Summer

Summer's selections turn away from self-reflection to embrace the great outside. They invite us to be confident of our place in the world, and of how we will navigate our own journeys, be that Nichols advising us how to cross a busy Delhi street or Thomas teaching us to appreciate a bright field. They are also joyful celebrations of natural beauty. The living is easy, and love is in the air.

The poems here invite nature's powers to heal us by giving us the words for all the wonder we can see but cannot express. They give us the images that mean that a tree or a flower can enter our consciousness in new and powerful ways, seared into our thoughts thanks to the alchemy of the poet's language. When we read a poem like Cummings's 'i thank You God for most this amazing', a tree is no longer just a tree. It comes alive as if it were a dancing crea-ture – 'Leaping greenly spirits'. And it comes alive in our minds too, expanding in significance and power through images that grab our attention with their vividness and truth to life. Thus is our ex-perience of the natural world enriched and deepened.

Summer's poems also offer us philosophical wisdom, about our place in the greater scheme of things. The poet's identifica-tion with nature is so profound he feels he is a part of something bigger. Spending time in nature triggers our appreciation, in Barrett Browning's words, for 'The Best Thing in the World', Summer's love-liness included. We leave behind Sexton's Winter despair, unable to belong anywhere and broken down into nothingness, and enjoy instead Wordsworth's celebration of the kinship which 'rolls through all things'.

Other writers here make the point that we can recall moments of natural beauty even when we are not in the countryside. Our conscious minds do not need to distinguish between real and imagined experience. We can always close our eyes and dream we are elsewhere, the sun smiling our gloom away, to paraphrase Bryant. These authors offer a peaceful reprieve from a sometimes oppressive present.

27.   'The Bright Field' by R.S. Thomas

I have seen the sun break through
to illuminate a small field
for a while, and gone my way
and forgotten it. But that was the
pearl of great price, the one field that had
treasure in it. I realise now
that I must give all that I have
to possess it. Life is not hurrying

on to a receding future, nor hankering after
an imagined past. It is the turning
aside like Moses to the miracle
of the lit bush, to a brightness
that seemed as transitory as your youth
once, but is the eternity that awaits you.

It is the silences at the end of each line that create the drama in this poem. The poet reveals his changing understanding of and connection to what matters: the bright field of the title.

In the first three-and-a-half lines, Thomas suggests a missed opportunity. He describes an everyday experience, of the sun breaking through clouds. The encounter did not grab his attention: he kept going and forgot it. Then comes his first realisation: that this mundane scene in fact was precious. The 'treasure', 'the pearl of great price' dwells in the apparent ordinariness of daily life. (The 'pearl of great price' comes from the Parable of the Pearl in the gospel of St Matthew and is a phrase that echoes through the literature of the Christian Middle Ages.) It is a reminder of how urgent and special this moment of interior revelation is – and yet so easy to overlook, like the bright field, as we rush, the emptiness of 'hurrying' suggested by the space between the first and second verse.

Thomas's second revelation is that what was precious has not been lost after all. He must still give 'all that I have' in response to natural beauty. The sunlight pouring on the field is like the light pouring from the biblical episode of the burning bush, leading naturally to an eternal brightness – 'lit bush' in Thomas's inspiring turn of phrase, rather than the more hackneyed burning. Given that the poet was an Anglican priest, it is possible that the bright field symbolises Christ.

Speaking with a gentle voice, as he admits he was misguided, Thomas is the perfect companion for when we undervalue or misjudge something but can embrace 'turning aside'. Here is the promise of a new and present brightness, right here, right now, there for the taking in our seemingly ordinary lives.

28.   'In the Mushroom Summer' by David Mason

Colorado turns Kyoto in a shower,
mist in the pines so thick the crows delight
(or seem to), winging in obscurity.
The ineffectual panic of a squirrel
who chattered at my passing gave me pause
to watch his Ponderosa come and go –
long needles scratching cloud. I'd summited
but knew it only by the wildflower meadow,
the muted harebells, paintbrush, gentian,
scattered among the locoweed and sage.
Today my grief abated like water soaking
underground, its scar a little path
of twigs and needles winding ahead of me
downhill to the next bend. Today I let
the rain soak through my shirt and was unharmed.

The first third of this poem sets the scene: a walker climbing the Colorado wooded hills in the misty rain (a Ponderosa is a tall, slender, North American pine). The atmosphere is uncertain: one minute we are in Colorado, the next in Japan; the crows only 'seem' to be delighted. The scene is also full of jittery movement: the squirrel is panicky; the Ponderosa sways; the long pine needles scratch the cloud.

But the mood becomes calmer when the narrator's journey uphill ends and he reaches the stillness of a wildflower meadow; though while he was walking he had no realisation he was so near the summit. Only then do we learn that the poet has been grieving. He does not say what for; only that today is the day his grief ends. The process feels inevitable and natural, like water disappearing into dry ground.

He likens his sadness to a wound that has left a scar. But the scar is not red and angry. Instead, in a metaphor that stops us with its strangeness, it is like a friendly downhill path, marked by twigs and needles. Grief helps Mason find his way; it isn't something to be afraid of, an idea that he suggests by referencing his rain-soaked shirt. On one level, the poet is literally soaked – he has established in the opening lines that he is walking during a shower. On another level, the rain is the outpouring of grief that allows him to feel. The sadness can no longer hurt him.

Mason's trek is both literal (through the hills) and metaphorical (through the process of grieving). In other words, we may be nearer the end of heartache than we realise; grief can guide us, and paradoxically bring its own relief. Nature gives Mason a new vocabulary, a means of interpreting his emotions and a reminder of how they can change. Meanwhile, Mason's poem keeps me company on my own walks. Of course the scenery is different from Colorado. But my feelings often echo Mason's as I tramp up and down the fells of the Lake District. It usually rains too.

29. 'Step by Step' by Kobayashi Issa, translated by Geoffrey Bownas and Anthony Thwaite

Step by step
up a summer mountain –
suddenly: the sea.

We take small steps into this small poem. Head bowed, not seeing much beyond the steps in front... But then a view of the ocean stretches out before us. Though compressed into three short lines, it's all there: the simple and striking combination of 'summer' with 'mountain' is enough for our imaginations to do the work for us. Less is more. We can feel the steady hot slog uphill, followed by a sudden panorama at the summit that makes it worthwhile; the refreshing breeze it brings.

Suddenly, there we are – wow! – looking at the view and savouring it; a reminder of how exhilarating taking on new challenges can be, whether that is literally climbing a mountain, or metaphorically embarking on any endeavour. I sometimes pin this poem on a notice-board near my desk when I begin work. Word by word, step by step.

The poem is also a reminder that the revelatory moment when we glimpse the sea can only come after patient and repetitive action over a long period: one is impossible without the other. The two experiences are inseparable, yes, but very different in feeling. By yoking the two together, and drawing the contrast between them, Issa makes both more vivid and appealing. And in doing so, he encourages us to take the first step, whatever challenge we are facing. A poem about finding our courage, then, and how good that can feel.

30. 'The Gladness of Nature'
by William Cullen Bryant

Is this a time to be cloudy and sad,
When our mother Nature laughs around;
When even the deep blue heavens look glad,
And gladness breathes from the blossoming ground?

There are notes of joy from the hang-bird and wren,
And the gossip of swallows through all the sky;
The ground-squirrel gaily chirps by his den,
And the wilding bee hums merrily by.

The clouds are at play in the azure space
And their shadows at play on the bright-green vale,
And here they stretch to the frolic chase,
And there they roll on the easy gale.

There's a dance of leaves in that aspen bower,
There's a titter of winds in that beechen tree,
There's a smile on the fruit, and a smile on the flower,
And a laugh from the brook that runs to the sea.

And look at the broad-faced sun, how he smiles
On the dewy earth that smiles in his ray,
On the leaping waters and gay young isles;
Ay, look, and he'll smile thy gloom away.

Bryant wills us to engage with Nature, personifying her as a laughing figure. Gladness too is personified, as breathing 'from the blossoming ground'. And so are swallows who gossip, clouds that play, leaves that dance, winds that titter, fruit that smiles. Nature literally comes alive, full of delightful characters with whom we want to connect.

This animated, joyful depiction dominates the poem, cancelling out the sadness and gloom of the first and last lines. The suggestion is that the power and intensity of nature's loveliness, encompassing the skies, the earth, the birds (a 'hang-bird' is an American bird that builds a hanging nest), the bees, the leaves, the wind, the brook and the sun, can by virtue of sheer abundance overwhelm something as slight and inconsequential as our low mood. If we adopt Bryant's sharp powers of observation and imagine nature in the way he does, we can become part of this delightful show, with the same potential for joy. (Indeed, numerous studies show that spending time in nature reduces stress, increases positive emotions and helps healing and concentration.) All we need do is look around us.

There is something especially heartfelt about Bryant's plea when we learn that his was an office-bound, city-dwelling life, as it is for so many of us. Even if we are not in the countryside in a literal sense, this poem can transport us there. We can adopt something of the lightness of touch and simple pleasure in existence that nature itself exhibits. At the very least, wherever we are, we can turn our faces to the 'broad-faced' sun, Bryant's invitation in the last verse, to smile our gloom away. A seemingly simple answer, but sometimes that is the best approach to the most intractable problems.

31. 'The Best Thing in the World' by Elizabeth Barrett Browning

What's the best thing in the world?
June-rose, by May-dew impearled;
Sweet south-wind, that means no rain;
Truth, not cruel to a friend;
Pleasure, not in haste to end;
Beauty, not self-decked and curled
Till its pride is over-plain;
Light, that never makes you wink;
Memory, that gives no pain;
Love, when, so, you're loved again.
What's the best thing in the world?
– Something out of it, I think.

Bracketed at the beginning and end with a rhetorical question, the poem immediately hooks the reader. What *is* the best thing in the world? For Barrett Browning the answer begins with images drawn from nature. The word 'impearled' has an old-fashioned feel about it; it does indeed go back to Middle English. Its literary feel contrasts with the rest of the poem's language, which is more down to earth, and fits the fantastical idea that the sun is busy creating jewels out of dewdrops on a rose petal.

Barrett Browning continues to give us more examples of what is best, personifying her ideas. We have the figure of Truth; then Pleasure; Beauty, and Memory. Herein lies Barrett Browning's subtlety: she knows that virtues can disguise vices. Each blessing comes with a qualifier. Each line here has got a 'no', a 'never' or a 'not' in it. The best thing in the world is truth – if it is *not* hurtful to a friend. Beauty, if it's natural and not adorned with makeup and an elaborate hairstyle, or curled hair. Love is the final thing Barrett Browning is grateful for and is a blessing that stands out by being treated differently. After the smooth-flowing earlier lines, 'Love, when, so, you're loved again' has a jumpiness to it, thanks to the commas and the word 'so', which make us pause and reflect. What does Barrett Browning mean? I understand 'again' to mean 'in addition': we are loved, anyway, but are loved over and above that too. By contrast to all the other blessings, there are no qualifiers to love.

The poem ends as it began with a rhetorical question. Does 'out of it' mean something taken out of her list in the poem? Or something taken 'out of this world', as in from things to be found on earth? Or are the wonders she describes due to some supernatural power, out of this world? Whichever interpretation speaks to you, there's something generous about this poem: by sharing what she loves, Barrett Browning invites us to do the same.

32. 'Advice on Crossing a Street in Delhi' by Grace Nichols

First take a few moments to observe
the traffic's wayward symmetry.

While contemplating wheels of mortality,
note how whole families on motorbikes
dart daring within the shifting shoal
of the cacophonous river.

Surely if they can, you too can
weave a quick trajectory
So go –
at the first signs of a small break
with a great faith and a great surrender.

If stranded in the middle of the road
become a sacred cow with gilded horns
adopting the inner stillness of the lotus posture.
Let honking cars, rickshaws, lorries,
swarm or fly around you.

You are in the hands of the great mother.
The thing about India maybe
is to get the rhythm right –
this rhythm that will change the way
you cross a street forever.

This poem has a strong, simple central image to hold on to: crossing a street in one of the world's largest and most densely urbanised areas, famed for its multidirectional traffic. This becomes an image for how to navigate life itself: something else that is busy, loud, full of danger but also adventure and joy. While the scene described is bustling, with a harsh, discordant mixture of sounds, the poet's tone of voice is soothing and sagacious by contrast. It is as if Nichols is holding our hand. We are, reassuringly, allowed to 'take a few moments' before we embark on our own journey.

The speaker places us readers in the position of tourists; perhaps like the speaker might have been herself one day, before she acquired the wisdom she is about to impart. We have newly arrived in a situation and are taken aback. Sometimes, when caught unawares by life, we too can seem like visitors to it: still naïve and shocked in the face of it. The example we are offered as a model of behaviour is 'whole families on motorbikes' who precariously and confidently make their way through the traffic, because they must. And if they can do it as a whole family, then we as individual pedestrians ought to manage, too.

How then do we navigate the poem, the street and life? We must observe the scene, but not wait too long before diving into the maelstrom: 'go – / at the first signs of a small break'. Nor must we imagine we can control everything – we must embark with a 'great surrender'. If we are momentarily overcome by life's chaos, we can instil a sense of control (albeit control over not being in control) by adopting the 'inner stillness' of a sacred cow, who, impossibly and laughably, has adopted the lotus position.

The suggestion is that humour is another clue to becoming an assured traveller. As is the idea of trusting that you are in the hands of 'the great mother' and getting the rhythm right. This last piece of advice is given most weight – if we only get the rhythm right, it will change the way we cross a street for ever. Each of us needs to find our own rhythm, our own pace that is inherent to each one of us. If we do so, then crossing the street is not so daunting after all. What was previously impossibly difficult now feels simple and easy.

33. 'i thank You God for most this amazing' by E. E. Cummings

i thank You God for most this amazing
day:for the leaping greenly spirits of trees
and a blue true dream of sky;and for everything
which is natural which is infinite which is yes

(i who have died am alive again today,
and this is the sun's birthday;this is the birth
day of life and of love and wings:and of the gay
great happening illimitably earth)

how should tasting touching hearing seeing
breathing any – lifted from the no
of all nothing – human merely being
doubt unimaginable You?

(now the ears of my ears awake and
now the eyes of my eyes are opened)

Here is a poet's gratitude for the unbridled wonder of God, expressed through the glory of nature. Cummings uses capitalisation deliberately to make this point. 'You' and 'God' emphasise God's power, and our insignificance ('i' is not capitalised). He stresses our human unimportance by his use of brackets in the second and last verses describing his personal awakening: throwing it off as though it were a mere aside.

Words are arranged in an illogical order, for example in the first line of the poem, which dislocates 'most'. He surprises us again in the third stanza when he adds the suffix 'ly' to the adjective 'mere', thereby turning 'being' from noun into verb. These reversals make us stop and think, and they surprise us, just as Cummings himself is freshly amazed by God. They also convey Cummings's child-like wonder: like a youngster, he seems to muddle his words.

There's significance, too, in the way Cummings eliminates the space after each colon and semicolon. Spaces would have given us a momentary pause. Instead, the speaker is breathless in his enthusiasm for the 'trees' and the 'sky', tumbling over his words (again like a child) in his rush to describe a nature full of spiritual wonder: the spirits of the trees and the dreams of the sky. God and nature merge in a medley of 'life and of love and wings', this pulsing energy relentless in lines such as 'the gay / great happening illimitably earth' and the quick, choppy beat of 'leaping greenly spirits of trees'.

By the final two lines, the poet is hearing and seeing in a different way thanks to God, who has awoken his inner or spiritual ear, and opened his spiritual eyes. Being close to God is what makes Cummings feel fully alive. Others may find this poem connects them to kind of a pure awareness, a life force pulsing through the universe that Cummings describes, but not feel it to be divine. Either way, Cummings gives us words for those heart-stopping moments of feeling fully human when the ears of our ears awake and eyes of our eyes are opened. Something deep-seated within our senses is activated, as if hitherto we only operated on the most surface level. A poem to make you feel more deeply alive.

34. 'Pied Beauty' by Gerard Manley Hopkins

Glory be to God for dappled things –
　For skies of couple-colour as a brinded cow;
　　　For rose-moles all in stipple upon trout that swim;
Fresh-firecoal chestnut-falls; finches' wings;
　Landscape plotted and pieced – fold, fallow, and plough;
　　　And áll trádes, their gear and tackle and trim.

All things counter, original, spare, strange;
　Whatever is fickle, freckled (who knows how?)
　　　With swift, slow; sweet, sour; adazzle, dim;
He fathers-forth whose beauty is past change:
　　　Praise him.

How do you evoke beauty? And how do you capture the beauty of movement – 'trout that swim' – with something as static as words? Hopkins does it by playing with language in a way that embodies this sense of flux; and through compound words such as 'couple-colour', 'rose-moles', 'chestnut-falls' and 'fresh-firecoal'. The effect is to speed up our reading: one action follows another in quick succession, to the point where we feel the world is constantly on the go.

Hopkins also brings beauty alive through his celebration of things that are 'pied', combining contrasting colours, often dark with light, whether in the sky, the freckled markings on a trout – stipple means speckled, brinded means patterned – the wings of finches or the ploughed landscape. For it is not just the natural world that shows God's glory – it is also human activity. Pied beauty can be found in the way that people work the land: think of green turf against the colour of brown soil, and the labour of humanity more generally.

Hopkins contrasts the fickle world with the unalterable world of God, who is 'past' or beyond change. But consider this: God is responsible for fathering all that beauty. The simple clarity of the imperative 'Praise him' in the last line resolves any uncertainty as to our own role: no fickleness there.

This poem was written relatively early in Hopkins's career. Later, he suffered and wrote about despair, as we have seen from his poem 'No Worst, There Is None' (see page 35). Perhaps there is some consolation in knowing the extraordinary joy he at least enjoyed at an earlier point in his life.

35.   'The Lake Isle of Innisfree' by William Butler Yeats

I will arise and go now, and go to Innisfree,
And a small cabin build there, of clay and wattles made:
Nine bean-rows will I have there, a hive for the honey-bee,
And live alone in the bee-loud glade.

And I shall have some peace there, for peace comes dropping slow,
Dropping from the veils of the morning to where the cricket sings;
There midnight's all a glimmer, and noon a purple glow,
And evening full of the linnet's wings.

I will arise and go now, for always night and day
I hear lake water lapping with low sounds by the shore;
While I stand on the roadway, or on the pavements grey,
I hear it in the deep heart's core.

The first line has an urgent and biblical feel, 'I will arise' being a common phrase in the King James Bible, and the repetition of 'go' lending certainty to the poet's plan. Yeats's journey is a literal and spiritual one, the mystical feel suggested by the spell-like repetition of 'build there', 'have there', 'have some peace there'.

The poet's life will be one of honest toil: building a cabin, planting beans and keeping honey bees. Life will quieten, as he lives amid his 'nine bean-rows' alone in 'the bee-loud glade', the long-drawn-out vowels evoking a languid tranquillity. The lull in pace is suggested by the shorter fourth line at the end of each stanza, allowing the reader to pause and linger. It is by slowing down to nature's pace that we find time for the elusive peace we seek. Peace and the early mist become one, dropping 'from the veils of the morning'.

By the last verse, we are there. We can hear the 'lake water lapping with low sounds', the repetition of words beginning with 'l' evoking the sound of the waves lapping too. The soporific mood only changes in the penultimate line, a reminder of the greyness and austerity of the city. Even so, Yeats is determined to remain true to his 'deep heart's core' – a struggle for all of us, yet one which he shows is worth pursuing because it offers the extraordinary gift of peace.

36. From 'Lines Written a Few Miles Above Tintern Abbey' by William Wordsworth

..... For I have learned
To look on nature, not as in the hour
Of thoughtless youth, but hearing oftentimes
The still, sad music of humanity,
Nor harsh nor grating, though of ample power
To chasten and subdue. And I have felt
A presence that disturbs me with the joy
Of elevated thoughts: a sense sublime
Of something far more deeply interfused,
Whose dwelling is the light of setting suns,
And the round ocean, and the living air,
And the blue sky, and in the mind of man –
A motion and a spirit that impels
All thinking things, all objects of all thought,
And rolls through all things. Therefore am I still
A lover of the meadows and the woods
And mountains, and of all that we behold
From this green earth; of all the mighty world
Of eye, and ear, both what they half create,
And what perceive; well pleased to recognise
In Nature and the language of the sense
The anchor of my purest thoughts, the nurse,
The guide, the guardian of my heart, and soul
Of all my moral being.

The poem was composed 'during a tour' of the Wye Valley, a few miles above the romantic ruins of Tintern Abbey, on 13 July 1798. The view looking down on the Abbey gives Wordsworth a perspective that he applies to his own life. It brings back memories of an earlier visit when he was a 'thoughtless youth'. But on this occasion, he experiences a spiritual encounter with his surroundings. He hears 'the still, sad music of humanity' and feels a mystical presence that imbues nature and the mind of man.

Wordsworth conveys this notion of connectivity so powerfully that it becomes believable, to the point where we can find it a consoling concept. We can follow his logic and experience the same connectivity, the feeling that we are part of something bigger. The poet evokes the transcendent purity and magic of this presence, which dwells in the 'light' of setting suns: the plural 'suns' is strange and compelling, as is the 'round ocean' and 'living' air. The kinship that 'rolls through all things' is also evoked by the repetition of 'and' – 'And the round ocean, and the living air.' Wordsworth manages to describe something as evanescent and philosophical as this relatedness with nature in such a way that it feels 'like an anchor'. Our spiritual voyage has been as real and grounded as Wordsworth's actual revisiting of Tintern Abbey.

Much had changed in Wordsworth's own life since he had first visited the Abbey. In between then and the writing of this poem, he had gone to live in France, stirred by the idea of that country's revolution. There he had a daughter with a French woman, Annette Vallon. But the political situation turned: the optimism of the revolutionary age soured, and Wordsworth's Englishness made him an object of suspicion. He was forced to leave France and his new family behind.

Now he can hear 'the still, sad music of humanity': he has a new awareness that allows him to see our suffering reflected in nature.

But this paradoxically brings him closer to nature: we are not separate from the natural world – rather it reflects all aspects of our being, including our sadness. Ultimately, feeling this connection means nature still can rescue him, and man in general, from his essential loneliness. The poem keeps us company, and so does the natural world – the nurse, the guide and the guardian of our hearts.

37. 'A Summer's Night' by Paul Laurence Dunbar

The night is dewy as a maiden's mouth,
The skies are bright as are a maiden's eyes,
Soft as a maiden's breath, the wind that flies
Up from the perfumed bosom of the South.
Like sentinels, the pines stand in the park;
And hither hastening like rakes that roam,
With lamps to light their wayward footsteps home,
The fire-flies come stagg'ring down the dark.

A sensual summer night is 'dewy as a maiden's mouth'. 'Dewy' is something we would more normally associate with the freshness of the early morning, but here the adjective conjures a moistness and expectation of romance in the night air. Meanwhile there is something medieval and a touch magical about the thrice repeated use of the word 'maiden'.

Dunbar extends this metaphor in the second line: the skies are as bright as a woman's eyes, while the wind is 'a maiden's breath'. Such arousing images: our sense of touch is awakened by the thought of the softness of the breath. Meanwhile the scented wind excites our sense of smell. With a picture of the wind blowing from the 'bosom' of the South, it's as if the landscape was alive: a person whose chest is rising and falling with each intake of breath. (South refers to the American South. Dunbar was born to parents who had been enslaved in Kentucky before the American Civil War, and later freed. Many of his poems evoke life in turn-of-the-century America.)

Then, in a park, the pines stand like guards keeping watch. And, like hellraising, womanising young men – an impression furthered by 'wayward' – fire-flies come 'stagg'ring' drunkenly 'down the dark', heading homewards after a night's hellraising, each with its own light. Throughout the poem, the alliteration, especially in the second verse (park', 'hither hastening', 'lamps to light'), adds a singsong feel to the words of a writer who in 1903 penned the lyrics of the first African American musical ever produced on Broadway. You could imagine this poem being put to music.

This poem reminds me of the intensity of my teenage years when I partied late into the summer nights. A part of me grieves the fact that those days are gone, but another part of me is relieved. Sensual, intense, dangerous: the poem reawakens those long-dormant feelings, but also a relief at their passing.

38. 'Fragment' from Sappho, translated by Josephine Balmer

Beauty endures only for as long as it can be seen;
goodness, beautiful today, will remain so tomorrow

The Ancient Greek poet Sappho argues that though the concept of outward 'beauty' is ephemeral, the same word can be re-invoked as an adjective, 'beautiful', and carry with it, in the second line, the idea of permanence attached to inward goodness. 'Beauty' and 'beautiful': such similar words but used here to convey something different in feeling.

Sappho's message that good endures is more powerful as it is conveyed with such simplicity. Two short lines conjure a whole philosophy: that integrity and goodness are in and of themselves beautiful, and indeed where real beauty lies, rather than in all the outward transient signs of loveliness that we see in the world – be that in others, or indeed in nature. Goodness is what will remain of us, not our fading looks. It is a message that I find reassuring and necessary whenever I find myself scrolling through my social media and becoming obsessed with outward signs of attractiveness.

What we write can also act as our legacy, just as our good deeds can outlive us. Sappho was born in the seventh century BC, and her poetry exists in fragments, each barely a few lines long, salvaged from scraps of ancient papyrus or saved by other writers who copied out her verse. Most come to us completely without context, as if they had been plucked from the middle of a poem. Part of the magic of these lines for me is that Sappho's work has survived over so many centuries. I feel connected to her across time. Our worlds are different, but what matters is the same.

39. 'Soapstone Retreat' by Mimi Khalvati

Late summer sun is falling through the forest.
As if the forest knew it would soon turn yellow,
it shifts a little, stars in the creek below
signalling to the sunlight on its crest.

In the centre it is still. Still late August.
On the periphery, branches, leaves, follow
the scent of autumn. Like a woodfire slow
to get going after the stove's long rest,

the forest stirs with ambivalent longings
for movement, stillness, as if its life were elsewhere
but its heart were here. And as cold nights near,

those last sweet sips at the cusp of the year
hang suspended in the balance as the flask swings,
hummingbird feeds and the sun sinks, stair by stair.

This poem seems completely in harmony with nature's rhythms. Its magic derives from the perfection of its description of a forest readying itself, reluctantly, for Autumn, just as we too ready ourselves for the turn in the season, finding it equally hard to let go of Summer's loveliness.

In the first verse, the forest is personified, preparing itself to 'turn yellow': all the poem's images operate as one interconnected organism: the yellow of the high sun is the colour the trees will soon turn. But the forest is a creature that 'shifts a little', as if it were slightly uncomfortable at what will soon befall it. This reluctance is suggested too in the line 'In the centre it is still': the forest has not yet fully accepted it is on the move: only the periphery is following the 'scent of autumn'. Likewise, the line 'Like a woodfire slow / to get going after the stove's long rest' signals a similar reluctance to shift into Autumn – the forest's longings are 'ambivalent'.

There is an inevitability to this change in the seasons: all the creatures of the forest kingdom know what is happening, yet there is an ambivalence too for what will be lost. In the third verse the forest longs for both 'movement' and 'stillness': an impossible contradiction.

By the final verse, the poet celebrates the ebbing away of the glory of Summer – 'those last sweet sips at the cusp of the year' – all the sweeter because we know them to be limited. The change of season is both sad and welcome. Just as when the autumn colours return, they are comforting without us having even realised we were going to need them. There is a sense of things having their moment and having *had* their moment.

There is certainly an air of stillness and solitude throughout the poem; time taken to reflect and appreciate the changing glories that nature offers us. The poem evokes a moment of perfect stasis even more poignantly because a change of season is imminent. If only we could be there: an impossibility, as the poem takes its name from a celebrated but now closed literary retreat set in woodland along the coast of Oregon.

AUTUMN
Time for Reflection

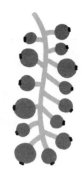

Introduction to Autumn

Autumn is a time to squirrel away the provisions we need for the privations of the Winter ahead. So the texts in this section are what I think of as golden nuggets of wisdom, to be reflected upon, and stored safely in my mind before the onslaught of darker days. Like drinking the last drops of a fine wine or lingering over the last few bites of a sumptuous meal, Autumn arrives on the heels of Summer, urging us to harvest the abundance and fill up with sweetness. All too soon, the light will be gone, the days will be short and the nights long. This is a time to gather up nature's bounty to keep alongside us in days ahead.

Many of the poems reflect insights that have enriched my own life. Often, just as I have begun to learn a lesson on some topic or other, I have then chanced upon words that reflect and make even more sense of the experience or sum up advice I wish I had known. If only I had come across the poem first, and absorbed its message, my life might have progressed more smoothly. But at least I now have some trusty lines I can rely on and find myself returning to often in my current everyday life. They feel like compasses, reminding me how to navigate through life's tricky landscapes.

Given their advisory nature, many of the pieces in this section do not require the same kind of textual analysis as the ones in other seasons, and some pack less of a visceral, emotional punch. Nevertheless, they have proved just as valuable in their way.

They feel as if they keep me protected: wise counsel to which I can turn, whether my mood is reflective and mellow like Autumn itself, or I need the perspective these words bring. Templates for living, when everything snaps into place.

It's easy to forget to look after yourself once the worst of the storm has passed. These pieces are here to help you feel calm throughout what Freud called 'ordinary human unhappiness'. Emily Brontë leads us into Autumn, arguing that we should welcome falling leaves and dying flowers and even death itself, while later on her sister Charlotte suggests that to be cheerful and full of hope is not to deny difficult times. Feay, in a poem written especially for this anthology, suggests that Autumn can be about new beginnings and evokes an unexpected delight at the end of Summer.

The following poems in this section become more philosophical, true to the reflective feel of the season. D'Aguiar suggests a world of endless plenty, Meanwhile, Carver argues that happiness is comprised of a multitude of moments, many of which often go unnoticed. I enjoy the simplicity of many of these passages and their direct address. Life is indeed a journey.

The hidden secret of Autumn is this: the leaves don't change colour. With the winter season coming, and without the key ingredients of warmth and sunshine, the trees begin to break down and lose their 'green', leaving the other colours that have been there all along – the magical reds, golds and oranges – to begin to emerge and express themselves.

Like these poems, there is something eternal and everlasting in this process: simply the dying back of the greenness that has been masking the tints inside. The beauty has been there all along. And we as human beings are like this, containing hidden jewels beneath the surface.

40. 'Fall, Leaves, Fall' by Emily Brontë

Fall, leaves, fall; die, flowers, away;
Lengthen night and shorten day;
Every leaf speaks bliss to me
Fluttering from the autumn tree.
I shall smile when wreaths of snow
Blossom where the rose should grow;
I shall sing when night's decay
Ushers in a drearier day.

Here Brontë orders nature about (as if it were alive and could respond to her instructions) with a child-like fierceness. We are instantly swept up by the urgency of her passion. Leaves are to fall, now! (the fall repeated twice); flowers must die. By the third line the poet's tone softens and turns inward to her own emotional connection with the falling leaves, and her deeply personal use of that word 'bliss'. Now each single leaf – so much more powerful than 'leaves' in the plural – is individually personified, communicating to Brontë. By the fourth line, the softening continues. 'Fall' has eased into the descriptive and gentle 'fluttering'.

The poet continues to luxuriate in being at one with the turn of the seasons, smiling and singing at the arrival of what we might usually think of as the negative harbingers of Winter: snow, night's decay, dreary days. Yet for Brontë these are things of beauty, exemplified by her image of 'wreaths of snow': what is so striking here is the way in which the language of Summer garlands is re-appropriated to describe Winter.

She uses language and rhyming couplets so simply that the sentiment that we should welcome autumnal decay, and indeed death, seems almost commonplace. This notion of the commonplace serves to reinforce the idea of the drearier day to which she looks forward. By the last line, the invitation is to us, the reader, to sing like her, instead of lamenting the coming of Autumn and Winter. Like Brontë, we can accept, allow and embrace each present moment in the cycle of life, welcoming what we might previously have dismissed as sad or negative. All feelings can speak to us, just as they speak to Brontë.

41.   'Revenant' by Suzi Feay

Twilight, tired traveller. The chapel on the hill
In parallax shifts its weight and twists about
As you slur down the track.
You dreamed of coming back.
Negotiating the cattle-grid's struts

Your heels strike chords through the dim air.
Pylons stride high, as you remember them
And there – the dragon's pool!
You let your last bag fall
As if enchanted and you cross the stream.

Up the dark drive. The lights pour on the lawn.
Rhododendrons confer and nod their heads.
You know it's always autumn here.
A fine mist in the air
Diffuses the sharp smell of musky, crushed, dead

Matter. Dark wanderer, you're home,
Your troubled summer over, work is done.
Open the door.
All you remember are there
All sinister, unchanged. And all of them are young.

Life drops fast from you now.
You're slipping back. You have a place, a name.
And then the bell.
Automatically you fall

In step and follow – and everything's the same.

The noticeboards are feathered full
Of paper sheaves. The hall floors gleam.
In the corridor you pass
A speckled looking-glass.
The years – all rubbed away. You're young and green.

A revenant can refer to someone returning from exile as well as someone who has returned from the dead in a physical body. Here Feay plays with both meanings. The protagonist is returning home, after a long journey. When she arrives, she finds something odd, indeed something 'sinister' about all the people she remembers. They are 'unchanged', still youthful, though they should presumably be different, as time has passed. Maybe they are ghosts? Or returned from the dead?

This ambiguity contrasts with the certainty of the delight the traveller finds in the fact that her Summer is over. Summer might more usually have more joyful connotations, but Feay reverses our expectation. Here it is Autumn that evokes peace and acceptance after the dramas of being away, a place where the 'tired traveller' can rest:

'.... Dark wanderer, you're home / Your troubled summer over, work is done.'

It is Autumn that is a place of enchantment and dragon's pools; of fine mists and welcoming shrubs; of lights pouring onto lawns. Feay draws out this unexpected delight in Autumn, a delight so powerful that it magically returns the traveller to her youth (her journey has been both literal and metaphorical). The last two verses evoke memories of the start of the Autumn term; of school bells, your name on a peg, your desk in the classroom, that feeling of belonging, the unthinking acceptance of rules, the falling 'in step', the noticeboards full, the hall floors shiny ahead of the arrival of hundreds of small children.

Throughout the poem, Feay conjures a feeling of profound presence in the face of great emptiness. We walk at the traveller's side, so vivid are Feay's images. They appeal to all our senses in turn. We can hear the clatter of her heels 'strike chords through the dim air'; we can visualise the personified rhododendrons conferring and nodding their heads; we can smell the scent of the house, a place where it's always 'autumn'; we can see the mirror with its green tarnish as the poem ends.

By the last line, the 'dark wanderer' has become 'young and green'. Paradoxically, while Autumn marks the approach of Winter and trees lose their leaves, in this poem it is also the season of new beginnings.

42. 'Lake and Maple' by Jane Hirshfield

I want to give myself
utterly
as this maple
that burned and burned
for three days without stinting
and then in two more
dropped off every leaf;
as this lake that,
no matter what comes
to its green-blue depths,
both takes and returns it.
In the still heart,
that refuses nothing,
the world is twice-born –
two earths wheeling,
two heavens,
two egrets reaching
down into subtraction;
even the fish
for an instant doubled,
before it is gone.
I want the fish.
I want the losing it all
when it rains and I want
the returning transparence.
I want the place
by the edge-flowers where
the shallow sand is deceptive,

where whatever
steps in must plunge,
and I want that plunging.
I want the ones
who come in secret to drink
only in early darkness,
and I want the ones
who are swallowed.
I want the way
the water sees without eyes,
hears without ears,
shivers without will or fear
at the gentlest touch.
I want it the way it
accepts the cold moonlight
and lets it pass,
the way it lets
all of it pass
without judgment or comment.
There is a lake,
Lalla Ded sang, no larger
than one seed of mustard,
that all things return to.
O heart, if you
will not, cannot, give me the lake,
then give me the song.

Many of us live in our heads, but here is a poem about a visceral desire to feel. We are caught up in the poet's urgency to live with a new intensity – 'I want, I want' – which mounts as the poem unfolds. It is an intensity that comes naturally to the 'maple / that burned and burned / for three days', which 'without stinting' allows the reddening of its leaves, even if that is agonising, as if the tree were on fire. And it is an intensity that is also experienced by the 'shallow sand', where 'whatever / steps in must plunge': the poet wants that 'plunging' too, even with its suggestion of violent penetration; or to feel as easily as water, that 'shivers without will or fear / at the gentlest touch'.

This fierce longing for sensation combines with something quieter: an acceptance of the letting go. Again, nature can be our guide. The leaves fall; the lake 'takes and returns' whatever 'comes to its green-blue depths'. For a moment there are two of everything as the placid waters reflect the earth, the sky, and the egrets, before the reflection passes. Then the lake's surface will alter again, shaken up by the rain, before its 'transparence' will return. Finally, towards the end of the poem the 'cold' moonlight will pass. In a similar way, things come and go in seasons of our own lives: relationships flourish and then wither; our work evolves; our identities deepen. Let us embrace these changes with ease. Let us know what it is like to lose everything, including the calm surface of the lake – 'I want the losing it all' – because only then can the stillness and composure return. Let us adopt something of nature's grateful acceptance of the whole movement of life itself, its ebb and flow, without judgement and no longer resisting change.

The poem ends with a last cry to Lalla Ded, a Kashmiri mystic and saint who lived in the fourteenth century and wrote poems and songs. One of her poems features a metaphorical lake no bigger than a mustard seed, deep within her heart. Even if we cannot know a real lake directly ourselves, let our hearts be filled with songs of trees and water, a reflecting echo of natural peace and tranquillity, there to nourish us and to teach us how to live. 'Then give me the song': shorthand I use in my daily life to remind me of this poem's wisdom.

43. 'Little Things' by Julia Abigail Fletcher Carney

Little drops of water,
Little grains of sand,
Make the mighty ocean
And the beauteous land.

And the little moments,
Humble though they be,
Make the mighty ages
Of eternity.

So our little errors
Lead the soul away
From the path of virtue
Far in sin to stray

Little deeds of kindness,
Little words of love,
Help to make earth happy
Like the Heaven above.

Small things can have a big impact. While a drop of water or grain of sand on its own might seem insignificant, added together they create oceans and lands. Equally, time is made up of slight moments, which together make up eternity.

Carney begins by using the example of the natural world, and moves on to the more philosophical nature of eternity. Then she applies the same logic (that the seemingly insignificant can be significant) to our errors. If we are unaware that even small wrongdoings can soon add up, we may, without realising it, be led astray. What began as one tiny wrong turn can lead to a very dark place.

But we can rest assured that the reverse is just as true. We can change this narrative of losing our path if we engage in kindness through little benevolent steps towards others. We can relax: together, they add up to something as transformational as making the earth happy.

Forget grand gestures. Carney's message is that these tiny, well-meaning steps are everything. She weaves these points together through the repetition of the word 'little' throughout. A small poem can have a big effect: Carney makes a powerful argument, disguised by a light touch.

44. 'Crossing' by Jericho Brown

The water is one thing, and one thing for miles.
The water is one thing, making this bridge
Built over the water another. Walk it
Early, walk it back when the day goes dim, everyone
Rising just to find a way toward rest again.
We work, start on one side of the day
Like a planet's only sun, our eyes straight
Until the flame sinks. The flame sinks. Thank God
I'm different. I've figured and counted. I'm not crossing
To cross back. I'm set
On something vast. It reaches
Long as the sea. I'm more than a conqueror, bigger
Than bravery. I don't march. I'm the one who leaps.

At the start of 'Crossing', Brown builds a world where we are trapped by endless repetition, both in nature and in our own lives. The natural world is described as having no variety, the water's sameness reinforced through the repetition of 'one thing'. A second instance, later in the poem, is the image of the flame sinking over and over, as the sun sets with mundane predictability. These two examples of monotony in the natural world bookend the monotony of human life, a life of repetitive walking: 'walk it / Early, walk it back' (the to-and fro-ing suggested by the line breaks). Existence just consists of 'rising to find a way to rest again'.

Yet this monotony is contrasted with a sunburst of self-affirm-ation later. 'Thank God', as the poet puts it, joy and confidence seem to emerge fully formed before we can even anticipate them starting to form. The poem issues an invitation to us to find our purpose, as well as a call to self-worth and self-acceptance.

Whereas others are trapped crossing and re-crossing the same featureless stretch of river, the poet has broken free from this cycle. He is now embarked on 'something vast', as vast as an ocean or sea in contrast to mere water. He is more than just an adventurer in this new universe: more than a conqueror, and 'bigger than bravery'. Not for him a life of repetitive marching, but instead one who 'leaps' into an entirely different realm.

'Crossing' has one last trick with the word 'one' and its repetition. At the start, it signifies constriction, homogeneity. By the end, it stands for individuality and freedom. We feel we too could become 'the one who leaps', so powerfully does the poet express the sense that there is a bigger world out there. We too can find 'something vast', something 'long as the sea'. His lines invite us to share his new optimistic mood. There is room for us too in this bigger world.

Brown wrote 'Crossing', he has said, during a state of depression in which he felt the only thing he could count on was his ability to write poetry. He took solace in the fact he could express himself in this way. We may not be writers, but we may be able to find our way of leaping, work that matters to us as much as poetry matters to Jericho Brown.

45.   'A Reverie' by Louisa Lawson

I am sitting by the river,
And I while an hour away,
Watching circles start and widen
In their momentary play.

Here a stronger whelms a weaker
As its ring expanding flies,
There one rises to the surface,
As another fades and dies.

And I solemn grow with thinking,
For just now it would me seem,
That each life is like a circle –
On time's deep, impellant stream.

Do we not upon its bosom
Linger for a little day,
Making faint and fleeting impress,
Then forever fade away.

While the strong unresting river
Toward Eternity doth glide,
All regardless of the circles
That have pulsed upon its tide.

As the speaker in this poem sits lost in thought on a riverbank, she comes to know from the ripples on the water something deeper about the nature of life and time: how we as individuals play our part in the larger scheme of things. We leave a 'faint and fleeting impress': but the shapes we have made are also beautiful and absorbing to witness. There is a second element to the metaphor: the river as time's 'deep, impellant stream', moving ever forward.

At first, her mood is simply reflective, as she observes the circles in the river at 'momentary play'. By the second stanza, her mood feels more melancholy, as she observes how brief is the life of each circle: each in turn is overwhelmed by a stronger circle, and 'fades and dies', with an inevitable sense of loss. By the third verse, she has become 'solemn', as she links the transience she sees before her with the transience of human life. We too make only the tiniest impression on the river of life, and we too then 'forever fade away'.

Yet there is consolation to be found in the final verse. Yes, we might feel our lives are insignificant, and will all too quickly be overwhelmed by something more powerful than we are. But the bigger ripple fades away too. This is the fate of all mankind, and as such we are united by our common humanity. Finally, there is comfort too in the sense that the river is 'strong' and 'unresting'. Whatever our individual insignificance, the river keeps running, gliding 'toward Eternity'. And we, it turns out, are part of that river, part of something much bigger than perhaps we realise. Our own eternity is assured as well.

46. 'Happiness' by Raymond Carver

So early it's still almost dark out.
I'm near the window with coffee,
and the usual early morning stuff
that passes for thought.
When I see the boy and his friend
walking up the road
to deliver the newspaper.
They wear caps and sweaters,
and one boy has a bag over his shoulder.
They are so happy
they aren't saying anything, these boys.
I think if they could, they would take
each other's arm.
It's early in the morning and they are doing this thing together.
They come on, slowly.
The sky is taking on light,
though the moon still hangs pale over the water.
Such beauty that for a minute
death and ambition, even love,
doesn't enter into this.
Happiness. It comes on
unexpectedly. And goes beyond, really,
any early morning talk about it.

How do you capture sudden, inexplicable happiness? In this poem, Carver distinguishes between his happiness as an observer and that of the boys he observes. They are absorbed in their task of delivering the papers and enjoying each other's company. There is no need for them to say anything, such is the extent of their mutual understanding and companionship, symbolised by their joint task and similar outfits. At the same time, the narrator describes how the simplest of moments – watching these two boys as he drinks his early morning coffee – can spark an unparalleled appreciation of life. The simplicity of the poem's wording and syntax and the absence of rhymes underline that sentiment, along with the easy informality right at the beginning in 'So early it's still almost dark out…'. We are right there with our downbeat, self-effacing narrator.

There are snatches of lyrical beauty too: the moon 'still hangs pale over the water'. That line hangs further out than any other into the water space, helping to create a scene of 'such beauty' that it can momentarily cancel out death, ambition and love.

At the end, we are back in the presence of the narrator, reminding us of his existence and ours on the periphery of this passing scene, closing the poem with the same matter-of-fact voice with which he began. It's a reminder that happiness and even its observation is fleeting. It 'comes on / unexpectedly' (the line break echoes the meaning) and is a reminder to us to appreciate small moments. When our children are under one roof, and everyone is more or less okay. When we laugh with a friend. When we watch the sun set, standing in a carpark. And simply accept them.

47. 'Love After Love' by Derek Walcott

The time will come
when, with elation
you will greet yourself arriving
at your own door, in your own mirror
and each will smile at the other's welcome,

and say, sit here. Eat.
You will love again the stranger who was your self.
Give wine. Give bread. Give back your heart
to itself, to the stranger who has loved you

all your life, whom you ignored
for another, who knows you by heart.
Take down the love letters from the bookshelf,

the photographs, the desperate notes,
peel your own image from the mirror.
Sit. Feast on your life.

Why is loving ourselves so hard? And how can we change this? Here, Walcott takes us by the hand and leads us not just to imagine but to believe in a new relationship with ourselves. We can relax right from the start of the poem, in the astonishing certainty that, in the future, we will greet ourselves with elation. It is only a matter of time.

Thus we can reverse the narrative that to love ourselves is selfish and wrong. It is natural, and normal, and should be part of our everyday lives: an ordinariness suggested by your 'own door' and your 'own mirror', and the gentle invocation to 'sit here. Eat.'

In case we slip back into our old ways of thinking, Walcott reinforces his certainty with the insistent and imperative 'will' in 'You will love again'. We need that certainty. We are so used to looking for ourselves where we are not, searching for the approval and esteem of our fellows and peers no matter what the cost to ourselves.

Instead, we can embrace unconditional love, just as Walcott embraces us. The frantic search for the approval of others is over. The poem ends with that same certainty. The simple instruction to 'sit' is a deliberate echo of Herbert's poem 'Love' (see page 68). But the poet's invitation is more than simply to eat; it is to feast. Here is a poem for the Autumn of our minds: a time to gather in and gorge on Walcott's message of self-love and acceptance, ready for any challenges that may lie ahead.

48. 'Autobiography in Five Short Chapters' by Portia Nelson

Chapter 1
I walk down the street.
There is a deep hole in the sidewalk
I fall in.
I am lost … I am helpless.
It isn't my fault.
It takes forever to find a way out.
Chapter 2
I walk down the same street.
There is a deep hole in the sidewalk.
I pretend I don't see it.
I fall in again.
I can't believe I'm in the same place
but, it isn't my fault.
It still takes a long time to get out.
Chapter 3
I walk down the same street.
There is a deep hole in the sidewalk.
I see it is there.
I still fall in … it's a habit.
My eyes are open
I know where I am
It is my fault
I get out immediately.
Chapter 4
I walk down the same street.
There is a deep hole in the sidewalk.

I walk around it.
Chapter 5
I walk down another street.

Change is possible. Nelson evokes this possibility by choosing something as simple as walking down a sidewalk (or pavement) as a metaphor for her journey through life. We all must walk down the street. The experience is universal, and so is change. However much we doubt our ability to act differently, Nelson shows that we can become more self-aware and take responsibility for our actions.

Whether she likes it or not, initially the poet keeps falling into the hole. There is comfort in this inevitability of learning, and the repetition is reassuring. The process is painful and takes time – we keep hurting ourselves by falling into holes; but Nelson is understanding, and we relate to her. She knows about bad habits; she understands our frustration at repeatedly making the same mistakes – 'I can't believe I'm in the same place'. Her journey is our journey. Her 'chapters' become increasingly short as the repetitive cycle is broken. Finally, she can embark on a new path, with the single-line stanza, full of possibility: 'I walk down another street'. This line is especially triumphant when we learn that Nelson wrote the poem in 1977, four years after recovering from breast cancer.

We need not stop walking. We need not move cities or continents or go travelling to learn from experience. We can keep doing what we routinely do, but with greater awareness and new perspective. It is not that Nelson stops walking; it is just that she chooses a different street. We finish the poem on a high, believing that we too can change.

49.   'The Border' by Fred D'Aguiar

Everybody took from a circle
What only arms could carry,
Yet this circle never depleted
As you would expect if people
Dipped into a bucket or a vault.

Instead it grew more pronounced
Seemed more circular if such a thing
Exists for a shape already manifest
Readymade for this world, all ready,
A whole world before those people

Gathered, their faces shining with
Conviction, for they know what they
Bring to the circle and what they take
From it, that no matter the exchange
That circle grows by giving them more.

This poem manages to take the abstract concept of boundlessness and make it real through the images it uses. We can instantly imagine people standing in a circle, helping themselves, though to what exactly we are not sure. Things aren't to be measured in terms of the everyday receptacles they fit into. (The 'vault' here calls to mind images of hoarding things away.) D'Aguiar's lines themselves have a roundness, a sense of running on and on, over-spilling: 'Yet this circle never depleted / As you would expect if people / Dipped into...' Just look at the line breaks here and throughout the poem, with sentences and thoughts fluidly passing between the lines.

While the first verse suggests a simple replenishing, by the second verse the concept is more ambitious. Now, the circle doesn't just replenish itself, but it expands – it becomes 'more circular' – a description that defies any usual logic, adding to a sense of magic. And we humans don't have to invent this circle or the plenty it provides. It is already in existence, part of the universe, and 'manifest / Readymade for this world, all ready...' By the third verse, there is a metaphorical richness to this sense of plenty. The people gathered round now have faces 'shining with / Conviction' as they too realise this astonishing secret of the universe.

We live in a world where it can feel as if there is never enough (and we feel we are never enough). We must compete for success, for money, for attention and popularity. These things make us prone to envy: to see someone else's achievement as taking from what we have. But this poem suggests another way: that there is more than enough for all. There is no scarcity. We do not need to hurry, because stocks will always last. The title of the poem seems to allude to precisely what it doesn't believe in, because here is a world without borders, either literal or metaphorical.

50. 'Life's a Journey'

And I think over again
My small adventures
When with a shore wind I drifted out
In my kayak
And I thought I was in danger.
My fears,
Those small ones
That I thought so big,
For all the vital things
I had to get and to reach.
And yet, there is only
One great thing.
The only thing.
To live to see in huts and journeys
The great day that dawns,
And the light that fills the world.

(Inuit prayer believed to have been written down by Knud Rasmussen on his Fifth Thule Expedition of 1921–1924. It would have been spoken in Inuit, written in Danish, and then later translated into English.)

How easy it is to misjudge what is important, this poem seems to be saying. We live in a state of fear and danger, pursuing what we imagine to be vital things. But we need not be so frantic. We need not do anything. Instead, we can continue to live our ordinary ongoing lives, with their 'huts and journeys', but are free to choose a different perspective. We can appreciate the gift that dawn brings every morning: that the world fills with light, something we are part of without even trying.

The context of this prayer is specific to a people and their habitat – most obviously signalled by the reference to drifting out in a kayak (the line drifts out too). But its appeal is that its message is universal.

What begins as a poem rooted in the narrator's local Inuit experience achieves this universality by broadening out at the end to encompass the whole world. We may not be preoccupied by our kayak drifting out to sea: our fears are different. But we too can enjoy effortlessly a simple belief in the light-filled world of which we are part, just as the Inuit are. This is conveyed by the simplicity of the language and shortness of the lines. We can enjoy the journey, without worrying about our arrival.

The peace we feel by the end means we find, to our surprise, that we connect with the Inuit (meaning simply 'the people') inhabiting certain regions of the Arctic. They might hitherto have seemed strange to us: their traditional beliefs include animism, the attribution of a living soul to plants and objects and a supernatural power that organises and animates the cosmos. But for now, we feel at one with them, as well as with ourselves and the universe.

This poem will always have a special resonance for me as it was one of the very last ones my mother shared with me before she died. Generous to the last, her hope was that I would worry less, and enjoy the great day that dawns.

51. 'Life' by Charlotte Brontë

Life, believe, is not a dream
So dark as sages say;
Oft a little morning rain
Foretells a pleasant day.
Sometimes there are clouds of gloom,
But these are transient all;
If the shower will make the roses bloom,
O why lament its fall?
Rapidly, merrily,
Life's sunny hours flit by,
Gratefully, cheerily
Enjoy them as they fly!
What though Death at times steps in,
And calls our Best away?
What though sorrow seems to win,
O'er hope, a heavy sway?
Yet Hope again elastic springs,
Unconquered, though she fell;
Still buoyant are her golden wings,
Still strong to bear us well.
Manfully, fearlessly,
The day of trial bear,
For gloriously, victoriously,
Can courage quell despair!

Some might find this poem naïve or overly optimistic. Yet therein lies its charm, Brontë deploying the light and playful touch that she promises us is the answer to life's challenges. With short lines, easy rhymes and pleasant images, she provokes in us a similarly light and pleasant mood. We can re-imagine life as no longer dark and full of gloom but filled with 'sunny hours'. Even Death is no match for the power of Hope, which bounces back like elastic, borne aloft on golden wings.

Brontë manages to combine this light touch with realism, which is why her words feel true to the spirit of proper courage. She has no illusions. To be cheerful and full of hope is not to deny difficult times, which after all she knew in her own eventful and challenging life: sorrow and joy are intertwined, and the one cannot thrive without the other – witness the rose blooming thanks to the rain. She further strengthens her point that we need a mix of lightness of heart and resilience by referencing how much willpower ('manfully') and courage ('fearlessly') hope needs to triumph. A mix of joy and toughness is required if we are to flourish. One without the other doesn't really work.

Combine them, though, and 'courage can quell despair'. Courage is a word that keeps popping up in my choice of poems: I am always struck by the word's derivation, from 'cor', the Latin word for heart. Courage originally meant to speak one's mind by revealing one's heart. Over time, this definition has changed, and courage is today more synonymous with being heroic. But I love its original meaning. Many of the poems in this anthology are about revealing one's heart, in the way that Brontë does here.

52. 'Desiderata' by Max Ehrmann

Go placidly amid the noise and haste,
and remember what peace there may be in silence.
As far as possible without surrender
be on good terms with all persons.
Speak your truth quietly and clearly;
and listen to others,
even the dull and ignorant;
they too have their story.

Avoid loud and aggressive persons,
they are vexations to the spirit.
If you compare yourself with others,
you may become vain and bitter;
for always there will be greater and lesser persons than yourself.
Enjoy your achievements as well as your plans.

Keep interested in your career, however humble;
it is a real possession in the changing fortunes of time.
Exercise caution in your business affairs;
for the world is full of trickery.
But let this not blind you to what virtue there is;
many persons strive for high ideals;
and everywhere life is full of heroism.

Be yourself.
Especially, do not feign affection.
Neither be cynical about love;
for in the face of all aridity and disenchantment

it is as perennial as the grass.

Take kindly the counsel of the years,
gracefully surrendering the things of youth.
Nurture strength of spirit to shield you in sudden misfortune.
But do not distress yourself with dark imaginings.
Many fears are born of fatigue and loneliness.
Beyond a wholesome discipline,
be gentle with yourself.

You are a child of the universe,
no less than the trees and the stars;
you have a right to be here.
And whether or not it is clear to you,
no doubt the universe is unfolding as it should.

Therefore be at peace with God,
whatever you conceive Him to be,
and whatever your labours and aspirations,
in the noisy confusion of life keep peace with your soul.

With all its sham, drudgery and broken dreams,
it is still a beautiful world.
Be cheerful. Strive to be happy.

Desiderata is the Latin for things that are desired or wanted, and in this poem the qualities of the soul and heart that we crave are laid out.

There is a timeless and universal feel to these words, and Ehrmann's message can appeal to us all regardless of our beliefs – as in the line 'Whatever you conceive Him (God) to be'. Its format as free verse gives a sense of unhurried calm: there are no undue embellishments in rhymes or rhythms to distract us from its messages about how to navigate life's path.

Ehrmann's advice is balanced and modest, and he quietly acknowledges the limitations of its application without sounding overly didactic. He is psychologically astute too, as in 'many fears are born of fatigue and loneliness'. His is a relatable and reassuring voice: he understands life's complexities, which cannot be reduced to absolutes.

What is absolute, however, is to recognise ourselves as much a part of the universe as the trees and the stars. The cosmos conspires to make things happen as they 'should', whether we understand the rationale or not. We are part of nature and the seasons, and Ehrmann's words are full of wise counsel to which we can turn whenever we need nurturing: an optimistic note on which to end this collection of poems and prose.

ENHANCING YOUR ENJOYMENT OF POETRY

Practical Ideas on Reading, Learning and Using Poems in Everyday Life

1.   Reading Poetry
2.   Memorising Poetry
3.   Writing Poetry
4.   Selecting Individual Inspiring Lines of Poetry

1. Reading Poetry

I was lucky in that an early familiarity with poetry has meant it is something I associate mainly with heartfelt pleasure, though of course there are plenty of poems that leave me cold, and plenty of others I do not feel I understand. How I experience a poem depends on my own inner rhythms: what I have been through that day, and my ever-changing moods. Probably the only thing that does not change is that I am not frightened of reading one.

For others, poetry can feel a bit daunting, something they disliked at school and which they have not returned to since. Here are some thoughts about how to read poetry in a way that may make it feel more approachable.

Start with the belief that poems can be a source of wisdom and beauty, open to anybody. Look at them as simply a way individuals have found to better convey moods and feelings that, can sometimes be so hard to pin down or find the right words for. Then, enjoy the fact that we as readers can relax: the poets are going to do the heavy lifting for us. We can just sit back and hear what the writers are telling us. Yes! we can say, that is exactly how sadness or joy feels, metaphorically punching the air.

This is the stage when we can benefit most from poetry's supportive properties. We feel our own state of mind has been understood and given expression. We are left feeling nurtured and supported and, crucially, less alone. Others understand us and have been there before us.

During this process, accept that poets use words in unusual ways to convey what they intend. Poetry tends to be different from other ways of writing, often using unusual interpretations, word order, punctuation and rhythm. These techniques give the poems pace, musicality, and emotion, sometimes enhanced by the poem's metre, or pattern of stressed and unstressed syllables, all of which add up to what the late poet P.J. Kavanagh called a 'tune' – something he felt all poems needed, as well as 'something surprising', his widow Kate Kavanagh told me. If this makes reading a poem sound more like hearing a song, well sometimes it is (though not every poem *has* to be thought of like a song: it's hard to 'hear' Raymond Carver in this way, or Jericho Brown, for example, but their poems are still enjoyable, and enjoyed). But at times if you think of it like that, the process can work its magic.

Given poetry's musical qualities, it follows that reading aloud can help your understanding of what the poet is trying to convey. You can hear another consciousness speaking in the poem's cadences of your own voice. You can feel the poem's rhythm in the way your fingers start tapping or your feet start pulsing. Reading the poem becomes a deeper, embodied experience.

Another strategy to squeeze the maximum meaning from a poem is to read the same one repeatedly, perhaps at night before you go to sleep, or again when you wake up in the morning. It's a trick others have found helpful. Just a few months before he died, Scott Fitzgerald wrote to his daughter Scottie about his experience of reading Keats's 'Ode on a Grecian Urn'. 'I suppose I've read it a hundred times,' Fitzgerald wrote. 'About the tenth time I began to know what it was about and caught the chime in it and the exquisite inner mechanics.' Sometimes we too need several readings to catch 'the chime' in a poem. I might stick a poem that I am getting to know on my bathroom mirror, to greet me as I start my day. Or I attach it to the fridge door. The poem offers a new flavour and feeling each time I read it, depending on my own state of mind. You may uncover nuggets that you had not noticed before.

A phrase or image may fall into place in a new way. I remember this once happening with Wordsworth's line 'The still, sad music of humanity' in his poem 'Tintern Abbey', and being struck by how the sound of the words reflected their meaning: I could hear what the music sounded like, thanks to the slow beat of 'still' and 'sad' followed by the speeding up in 'of humanity'. It was such a comfort to find a phrase that acknowledged life's complexity, its sadness, yet its music too.

A poem unfolds slowly, almost as if it is a present that you gradually unwrap, each layer of wrapping inviting new thoughts and responses. A brilliant poem is a present that keeps on giving. As readers we are given a gift, for us to do what we like with. And we can take what we need from that gift at any stage in our emotional lives.

Poets want us to benefit from their insights and the effort they have put into expressing them. They are artists who rarely wish to be intimidating or confusing. They want to talk to us and be heard. As the American poet Muriel Rukeyser once said: 'This moment is real, this moment is what we have, this moment in which we face each other, and if a poem is any damn good at all, it invites you to bring your whole life to that moment, and we are good poets inasmuch as we bring that invitation to you, and you are good readers inasmuch as you bring your whole life.'

In that sense, poets are no different from any of us, longing to communicate and connect. Yet while poets are like us, they have a particular gift: they can be blessed with extraordinary ways of putting feelings into words. You may not match their linguistic skill, but you will have much in common with them. By thinking about poets in this way, you may begin to feel you have a new circle of companions, friends even, as you navigate life's vicissitudes and the changing of the seasons, both inwardly and outwardly. A network of thinkers and philosophers have faced similar challenges to you, and in many cases have found answers, beautifully expressed, and packaged for our benefit. (For more on the lives of the writers quoted in this anthology, see pages 180–215.) If you persevere, you may be surprised at how many new friends you make, who have welcomed you into their world. Think of this new world as a sophisticated book club, which you may not have realised even existed, and of which you are now a part. Welcome, and let yourself be embraced.

2. Memorising Poetry

Poetry derives from a singing and oral tradition. Before the invention of writing, and in some societies long after it, the only way to pass on stories, poems or fables from one generation to another was through memorising and reciting them.

This tradition dates to man's earliest days. By the time of the Ancient Greeks, poetry was the foundation of their teaching methods: at social gatherings, people recited stories of their history and tales of ancient Greek gods and goddesses in long, rhythmic narratives.

In the later Middle Ages, learning poetry by heart was part of a noble's education. By the sixteenth and seventeenth centuries, memorising poetry was a tool used to improve people's memory and better their knowledge of the Bible. It was common for educated people to learn large swathes of text. By the beginning of the nineteenth century, reciting poetry in class was seen as important because it improved self-confidence, delivery and elocution. As time wore on, benefits such as self-discipline, physical awareness and posture were all added to the mix. Between roughly 1875 and 1950, recitation held a sizeable slot in school curriculums in America and Britain, but it has since largely gone out of fashion.

So there is a long history of the value of memorising poetry. And I have found it invaluable. Learning by heart the kinds of emotionally companionable poems you will find in this book may help you to engage even more closely with the emotions they evoke, without the distraction of the printed page. Your feelings, and the way the words work on them, can merge, the two becoming embedded in your psyche. There you may find some answers to those feelings, ways of negotiating them and truths that can help.

That way, you take the poem inside you into your brain chemistry, and you know the poem at a deeper, bodily level than if you just read it off the page. Through learning by heart, your own heart feels the rhythms of the poem, almost as if they were echoes or variations of your own heartbeat.

When I'm learning a poem, I remind myself that it is my own voice that is reciting the poem: it is just me talking, not anybody else, and I can try to find a voice that is both comforting and inspiring.

That voice can be summoned at will, whenever we need it. We have a rich mental resource right inside us, without having to find the poem in a book or on our phone. It is as if you have taken ownership of a piece of poetic landscape, one that you will always be able to revisit and roam in: somewhere we can go to whenever we want, whether it is in the middle of the night – Fitzgerald's 'three o'clock in the morning' – or when stuck waiting somewhere.

Memorising the poems in this anthology may help to enhance your understanding of the poems themselves: some of them take time to fully offer up their gifts, as we established in the previous section. And you are less likely to miss any hidden riches. The imprint on our consciousness will be that much deeper. The effort and time involved – and memorising is hard, given the complexity of many poems – contrasts with today's culture where search engines mean never having to rely on memory.

The advantages of learning some of the poems in this anthology by heart only work, I find, if you really know the words inside out, upside down, backwards, and forwards. Otherwise, there's room for anxiety. What was that line? Did I misremember it? And that gets in the way of all the benefits of memorising. In fact, I know very few poems off by heart, barely a dozen, and these I know so well that I can recite them with no worry at all.

My mental treasury of verse alters over the years: the poems I connect with change as I change. As I've said, probably the poem I turn to most in my memory bank is George Herbert's 'Love'. I have a limitless appetite for hearing its message that we are lovable and acceptable, and do not need to think of ourselves as 'unworthy and ungrateful'.

Choose a poem in this book that connects with your emotions in a similar way. The more you connect with that feeling, the more likely you are to be able to learn it off by heart. It's like music; the songs we find ourselves humming are the ones that have struck a chord within. Find the words that make you feel deeply.

Take your time to get to know and understand the poem. Read it aloud a few times, write it out several times, and look up words you do not understand. You may like to try to make connections between verses or stanzas by creating a storyline or outline in your mind. Studies show that our memories work better when we create such vivid images. Bite-sized chunks are advisable. Learn one or two lines at a time. Use opportunities such as walking, travelling or eating your breakfast to do this. Each time you memorise a new line, recite the whole poem from the beginning. The best way to learn anything is to expose yourself to it as much as possible, so keep repeating it.

Think about recording yourself reciting the poem on your phone, and then play the recording back to check you got all the lines right. Once you think you have learnt the whole poem, recite it frequently when it isn't to hand.

Finally, you may be thinking that one of the great joys of memorising poetry is being able to recite it to others. Whether to your children round the breakfast table, your colleagues at work or among a group of friends, the temptation is to challenge yourself to recite your poem clearly and passionately and to project your voice. And yes, this can indeed be a wonderful way to share your enthusiasm in a generous way, so that others too may find a poem inspiring. But do not feel you have to declaim a poem just because you have learnt it by heart. Performance anxiety might get in the way of your own enjoyment. For me, memorising a poem is generally more about talking to myself, rather than to others (though that can be fun too).

3. Writing Poetry

Full disclosure: I don't often write poetry, perhaps only once or twice a year. So I understand if you might never have considered writing a poem, and indeed the very thought could make you want to turn this page. But studies have linked good psychological health with creativity.

In the same way that an artist spills their feelings on to the page, writing a poem can pin down good times, so you can return to them later. Writing can also help make sense of adversity and anaesthetise trauma. I would never call myself a poet, but from time to time I jot down my thoughts in a poetic rather than prose format. I find this is especially true if I am feeling low or confused. My head may be full of difficult chaotic thoughts, but it all lessens when I get my thoughts on to the page. At least I have created something concrete and tangible when before there was just a swirling and shapeless darkness in my mind. You might also be inspired by reading other people's poems. This also often happens to those who come to my workshops. They came to enjoy reading poetry, but often they find they want to write it themselves by the time the sessions have ended, by which point I like to think that poetry generally feels more accessible and relevant and something they can try their hand at too.

Write straight from the heart: poetry is about conveying your feelings through the words you choose and the images they suggest. Sometimes a feeling is physical, held somewhere in the body. Sometimes it is suggested by a simple phrase. In a poem I wrote about my mother, I tried to recall her unselfishness, and her desire that others should not worry about her impending death, using the refrain she often used, 'I've had a good run.' Sometimes a particular emotion rouses a strong image. Recently, for example, a boy in a yellow T-shirt flying a kite summed up happiness on a trip to the park.

Before you begin… Notice when and how you feel creative. Overall, this should be a positive experience. If you begin to feel stressed, pause, do something else, and come back to the page. If you write from a place of joyful flow, your poem is likely to read better. And even if you are feeling low, taking time to seek out words to describe and make sense of your mood could prove a helpful distraction from the distress of the here and now.

If the thought of writing a poem still daunts you, make the process less agonising by giving yourself a time limit of say ten minutes or so. Don't worry about rhyming, and certainly don't worry about whether the poem is any good. It's better to get something down than agonise over what you are trying to say. Write first, worry second.

Here are some prompts I have used in my own poetry workshops, for those who wish to have a go at writing a poem. Take note of whatever is happening for you in this moment. Is your head full of thoughts? Is something you are seeing or smelling taking centre stage? Do you feel the emotion somewhere in your body? What sort of feeling? Does it have a colour or shape? Does it make a sound? Is there a particular image that occurs to you, or a line of dialogue, that sums up your feeling? You could use this first line as a prompt: the sky darkened; or, the sky lightened…

Could you create two people in your poem to discuss whatever dilemma it is you are writing about? This is particularly helpful when I am trying to make sense of something troubling, I find. One character can personify whatever is bothering you; the other is a character you identify with. Write a poetic dialogue between them.

If you find it easier, you could use the structure of an acrostic poem to help give your poem form, writing down a word vertically. Then use each letter as a prompt for the word that begins that line of your poem. If a poem doesn't come naturally, it doesn't matter. You could try jotting down a simple line that expresses how you are feeling instead. And if you are still suffering from writer's block, set a timer for three minutes and write continuously – about anything and everything – to help generate ideas. You may well feel pleased afterwards.

4. Selecting Individual Inspiring Lines of Poetry

I enjoy jotting down my favourite lines of poetry on cards, so I have them to hand, slipped in a pocket or bag as aides-memoires. Sometimes I prop the cards up on a bathroom mirror or by my computer – pocket reminders of feelings or approaches that can be helpful. For example, Milton's 'The mind is its own place, and in itself / Can make a Heaven of Hell, a Hell of Heaven' reminds me of the power of thought, and how by changing what we think we can change how we feel. And I reflect on the truth of Susan Coolidge's line that 'Yesterday's wounds, which smarted and bled / Are healed with the healing which night has shed.'

Other favourite sayings calm me down: reassuring messages such as Ehrmann's conviction that all of us are children of the universe 'no less than the trees and the stars; you have a right to be here'; or Hammerstein's promise that if we 'Walk on, walk on with hope in your heart / ... you'll never walk alone'. Some are simple calls to action, good for days when motivation deserts me: Gaskell's 'Do something' comes to mind. Or they amplify that glorious feeling of being at one with nature: Wordsworth's 'A motion and a spirit that impels/ All thinking things, all objects of all thought,/ And rolls through all things.'

Try coding your cue cards to highlight moods or emotions. Perhaps feeling 'anxious' or 'worried' in one; elated or joyful in another; needing hope or inspiration in a third.

My cards are now worn down and well loved. I carry them around with me. If I am feeling on edge, they feel like a security blanket. Just knowing that I have them in my bag gives me confidence. The words on each cue card are powerful memories from the poems in this anthology. Remember to bring the cards out when needed: don't leave home without them.

BIOGRAPHIES

Winter Writers

1. STEVIE SMITH (1902–1971)

Smith battled with depression. Other poets who also struggled with mental illness, like Sylvia Plath, who described herself as a 'Smith-addict', were drawn to her work. Born Florence Margaret Smith in Yorkshire, she was given the nickname 'Stevie' because of her likeness to jockey Steve Donoghue. When she was five, Smith fell ill with tuberculous peritonitis and was sent to hospital for three years. Her mother died when she was sixteen, which may partly account for Smith's preoccupation with death. After her mother fell ill, she was largely brought up by her spinster aunt Madge Spear, an inspiring figure whom Smith called 'The Lion'. Her job of thirty years was as a secretary, and she led an outwardly uneventful life behind the curtains of suburbia. By the 1960s, however, she had built a reputation as a performer of her own work, half-singing some of her poems in a quavering voice, playing up her reputation for eccentricity.

2. F. SCOTT FITZGERALD (1896–1940)

Fitzgerald was named after his famous if distantly related ancestor Francis Scott Key, the lawyer and writer who penned the lyrics to America's national anthem the 'The Star-Spangled Banner'. He was known to enjoy the family connection. Once driving past a statue of Key, while drunk, he supposedly hopped from the car and hid in the bushes, yelling to a friend, 'Don't let Frank see me drunk.' Best known for his novel *The Great Gatsby*, Fitzgerald was an unlikely success as a novelist, essayist and short-story writer: he was a poor student and atrocious speller who was nearly thrown out of Princeton. He never lived in the same place for more than a few years, his hard-partying lifestyle accompanying him wherever he went. Fitzgerald suffered from low mood and alcoholism, while his wife Zelda, considered the quintessential flapper of the 1920s, spent the latter part of her life in and out of sanatoriums. He never used the word 'depression'; instead, he described his mental state through metaphors, saying he was 'cracked like an old plate'. He ended his days in Hollywood, freelancing for the five big movie studios, and writing a Hollywood novel. He died just before Christmas in 1940, sitting in an armchair reading the Princeton alumni magazine.

3. JOHN BERRYMAN (1914–1972)

When Berryman was twelve, his father shot himself outside his window, an event that was to haunt him all his life. His family then moved twice, ending up in New York where his mother married a banker who adopted Berryman and his brother. They dropped their father's name of Smith and became Berryman. Berryman was as much a scholar and professor as a poet. He studied Shakespeare at Columbia and Clare College, Cambridge, and went on to teach at universities including Harvard, Princeton and Minnesota. His masterpiece, *The Dream Songs*, was awarded all the major American literary prizes and his influence on other poets like Anne Sexton was considerable. An anguished character, he married three times, suffered from a nervous temperament as well as alcoholism, and ultimately took his own life in 1972 when he jumped off a Minneapolis bridge in the dead of winter.

4. ABRAHAM LINCOLN (1809–1865)

Born in a log cabin in Kentucky, Lincoln spent his early years in Indiana. His mother died from drinking poisoned milk when Abraham was nine. Lincoln was president of the United States from 1861 until his assassination in 1865. He was keenly interested in the artillery used by his Union troops during the Civil War, test-firing muskets and rifles on the grassy lawns round the White House. Throughout his twenties and thirties, Lincoln suffered from what would probably now be called depression. He displayed suicidal tendencies: an unsigned poem, 'The Suicide's Soliloquy' is, generally, thought to be by him. He enacted the Emancipation Proclamation in 1863 that declared slaves forever free within the Confederacy; it was ratified in 1865 as the Thirteenth Amendment. Hours before his assassination at Ford's Theatre in Washington, he established the US Secret Service.

5. GERARD MANLEY HOPKINS (1844–1889)

Hopkins won a scholarship to Balliol College, Oxford, where he took a double first in Classics. In due course, he converted to Roman Catholicism and became a Jesuit priest. At this stage, feeling that writing poetry was too self-indulgent, he burned his early poems and devoted himself to study and teaching. Encouraged by his superiors, he returned to poetry, but his religious life was ever present. 'Pied Beauty' is framed by the English of the Latin phrases *Ad maiorem Dei Gloriam* (to the Glory of God) at the head, *Laus semper Gloriam* (praise God always) at the end, which are always used by students in Jesuit schools. He worked as a parish priest in Oxford and Liverpool but was always drawn to the countryside. Writing in the city became increasingly difficult for Hopkins: 'time and spirit are wanting,' he wrote, 'one is so harried and gallied up and down.' Soon afterwards, Hopkins moved to a university job in Dublin, which he hated. The tone of his poetry reflected his depression and eventually he dried up, deeply conflicted as he was by his religious obligations and artistic bent. In 1889 he died of typhoid fever, aged forty-four. Few of his poems had been published in his lifetime, but years later, at the age of ninety-eight, Hopkins's mother was presented with a book of the poems written by her son, who had been dead for twenty-nine years.

6. JOHN CLARE (1793–1864)

Born in Northamptonshire, Clare was an agricultural labourer. He stopped going to school when he was twelve and began working on the land in an attempt to help his parents pay the rent. He also began writing poetry about rural life, reading his verse to his parents under the guise of reading the works of another poet. He threw away what they didn't like and kept what they did. His writing initially brought him great success but left him conflicted: he was torn between the literary world of London and his need to take care of his family and seven children. By the late 1830s, his literary star was waning. A return to obscurity, a romantic break-up and the sense that he had become alienated from his rural roots exacerbated his tendency to depression. His doctors by contrast blamed his anxiety of mind on 'years addicted to poetical prosing'. By 1841, he was an inmate at the Northampton General Lunatic Asylum, where his symptoms worsened, and where he was to stay for the rest of his life. Luckily for us, his poetic impulse was unquenched while he was there, and he wrote some of his best poetry while incarcerated. When unwell, he believed he was a prize fighter with two wives. Later he claimed he was Lord Byron. He died of a stroke in 1864, when he was seventy.

7. PELE COX (1971–)
Pele was born in North London and named after the Brazilian footballer. She was accepted onto Andrew Motion's Creative Writing MA at the University of East Anglia – one of the first poets there – and, spurred on by his inspiring teaching and her love of Emily Dickinson's verse, she returned to London, reciting her poems to art dealers and artists at gallery launch parties. In 2013 she was appointed Poet in Residence at the Royal Academy of Arts and became immersed in the connection between poetry and the great artists. She also became Poet in Residence on the show 'The Naked Short Club', dedicated to the world of finance: she would read her poems in between hedge funders' reflections on the economy. It was here that she met a hedge funder who inspired her most well-known collection, *The Mistress Account*. This cycle of poems charts an affair from the perspective of the scapegoated mistress and was received to great acclaim at the Cheltenham Literature Festival in 2015.

8. AFRICAN AMERICAN SPIRITUALS
'Sometimes I Feel Like a Motherless Child' is a traditional folk song known as an African American spiritual, invented and sung by enslaved people on plantations. The songs were originally unaccompanied by music, created solely by a chorus of voices in a field, cabin or hollow. Typically, they were about the extreme hardships of being held in bondage, combined with elements from Africa's cultural heritage. Many spirituals were also rooted in Biblical stories, combining African musical traditions with European Christian hymns.

At first, major studios only recorded white musicians performing spirituals. That changed with the success of the African American blues singer Mamie Smith in the 1920s. African American composers and musicians began recording new spirituals. They remain at the heart of our attempt to understand slavery. Hearing these oldest musical expressions of the experience of enslaved people in America allows us, in Douglass's words, to understand something of the 'horrible character of slavery', more 'than the reading of whole volumes of philosophy on the subject could do'.

9. HELEN WADDELL (1889–1965)

Helen Waddell was an Irish historian who wrote a series of scholarly books on Catholic medieval Europe and enjoyed academic praise as well as popular appeal. Her books include *The Wandering Scholars*, *Medieval Latin Lyrics*, *Peter Abelard* and *The Desert Fathers* (featured here). The youngest of ten children, a poet, translator and playwright, she was born in Tokyo in 1889. When she was eleven, the family returned to Belfast, where she went to school and university. She was acclaimed for her study of medieval Latin poets, culminating in her book *The Wandering Scholars*, which analyses medieval Latin lyric poetry and the goliards, writers of satirical Latin poetry in the twelfth and thirteenth centuries. She died aged sixty from a debilitating neurological disease.

10. ANNE SEXTON (1928–1974)

A fashion model during the 1940s who liked to smoke menthol cigarettes, Sexton was an American poet much fêted in her lifetime. The daughter of a successful businessman, she was born in Newton, Massachusetts. Her childhood was materially comfortable but unhappy; relationships with her parents were difficult, possibly even abusive, and her closest confidante was her maiden great-aunt. She attended boarding school, and after graduation enrolled at a college in Boston that she later described as a 'finishing school', going on to teach at high schools, mental institutions, colleges and universities. Married at nineteen, she suffered a series of mental breakdowns following the birth of her first child in 1953, and her second in 1955. Her therapist encouraged her to write, which helped with her psychiatric struggles. She once wrote that 'everyone said: "You can't write this way. It's too personal; it's confessional; you can't write this Anne," and everyone was discouraging me.' She said she found the courage to write notwithstanding her critics because of the example of other poets, including Robert Lowell and John Berryman (see page 181). She took her own life at the age of forty-five.

11. JOHANN WOLFGANG VON GOETHE (1749–1832)

Born in Frankfurt, Germany, Goethe was a poet, playwright and novelist. He had a classical education and went to Leipzig University in 1765 to study Law. He earned accolades for his poetry and, at twenty-four, he wrote his novel *The Sorrows of Young Werther*, thought to have been responsible for a suicide craze across Europe. Men throughout the continent became gripped by Werther fever, dressing in the same way as the novel's eponymous hero. Such was the threat of further copycat suicides that the book was banned in several countries, including Italy and Denmark. In 1768 Goethe suffered a severe lung infection and spent a year and a half convalescing, during which time he wrote a series of ten poems set to melodies. In 1775, he dedicated himself to scientific and metaphysical studies at the royal Weimar Court before returning to poetry.

12. TISHANI DOSHI (1975–)

The poet and novelist Tishani Doshi was born in Chennai, then known as Madras, to a Welsh mother and Gujarati father. As a student she moved to America, where she discovered contemporary poetry by – among others – Mary Oliver, whose poem 'Wild Geese' is also in this collection. She then began writing: her book *Countries of the Body* (2006) won her the Forward Poetry Prize for best debut collection. Since her twenties she has also been a dancer, and movement often informs or inspires her poetry collections: two of them are dedicated to her mentor, the controversial Indian dancer Chandralekha, who died in 2007 and was known for her choreography that celebrated the human body. Doshi's work has explored the lives of women in India who have suffered violence at the hands of men, she dedicated a poem in her most recent collection, *Girls Are Coming Out of the Woods*, to her friend Monika Ghurde, whose rape and murder made headlines in 2016. The collection was shortlisted for the 2018 Ted Hughes Prize. Alongside her acclaimed poetry, Doshi has published three novels. Her most recent, *Small Days and Nights*, explores the attitudes of different societies towards differently abled people, drawing on the experience of having a brother living with Down's Syndrome. She currently lives in the south of India.

13. JOHN KEATS (1795–1821)

Keats's father Thomas was a livery stable keeper who died of an accident when Keats was eight years old. He made several medical connections through his grandmother, with whom he and his siblings lived before her death when Keats was nineteen. Through these connections, Keats began an apprenticeship in medicine, and eventually became a surgical assistant at Guy's Hospital. In 1816, he received an apothecary's licence, but chose to pursue poetry instead. According to a friend, Richard Woodhouse, Keats was unskilled at reading his own poems, not doing them justice. Always self-critical, he considered his earlier works to be so awful that he burned the lot. When Keats found out that his brother Tom had tuberculosis, he nursed him, putting his medical skills to use. Tom died in December 1817 and, unknown to Keats, he himself had caught the disease from his brother. Soon after his brother's death, Keats became engaged to Fanny Brawne and for the next year he produced the greatest of his works. The pair never married: he wanted to build his poetic reputation and become more financially successful before entering into matrimony. When Keats fell ill with tuberculosis he and Brawne could not have any physical contact; they communicated through a glass screen and sent each other love letters. Keats died when he was just twenty-five, in Rome, on 23 February 1821, of the disease that had also killed his uncle, mother and brother. He is buried at the Protestant Cemetery in Rome.

Spring Writers

14. MATSUO BASHŌ (1644–1694)

Born Matsuo Kinsaku, Bashō came from minor gentry in Japan. As a youth he was apprenticed to a samurai under whom he also studied to be a poet. It seems he never attained the rank of samurai himself. Upon the death of his master, he instead moved to the city of Edo, now Tokyo, where he further studied poetry and acquired a following of urbane, aristocratic students. He wrote of his desire for and affairs with his male disciples, and was considered among the first rank of the city's writers. Bashō wasn't to remain happy with city life. Seeking solitude, he took perilous routes into the wilderness that were then barely ever travelled alone. He took trips to Mount Fuji, Kyoto, Osaka and what he called 'the deep north', with periods of teaching in Edo. Towards the end of the eighteenth century, he was deified, and it became a crime in Japan to criticise his work. When he began, haiku (then known as hokku) was seen as more of a refined cultural pursuit than a respected art form. After he embraced this literary form, everything changed, and thereafter the haiku form became widely associated with nature.

15. EMILY DICKINSON (1830–1886)

Born into a prominent East Coast family in Amherst, Massachusetts, Dickinson spent most of her adult life isolated from the world, apart from brief attendance at a women's college for a year. She returned to her parents' home in 1848, perhaps due to anxiety, or agoraphobia; historians are not exactly sure why she subsequently withdrew from the world. Her mother had an episode of severe depression in 1855, and Dickinson wrote in a letter in 1862 that she herself experienced 'a terror' about which she could not tell anyone. The reclusive Dickinson wrote prolifically, composing thousands of poems, and preferred writing to company, rarely leaving home as she got older, and writing to friends rather than seeing them. She was also an enthusiastic gardener, growing flowers and vegetables, and overseeing the family's greenhouse full of jasmine, gardenias, carnations and ferns. Only a few of Dickinson's poems were published in her lifetime; not until the late 1920s did her poetry start to gain public recognition, and not until 1955 was a complete volume of her unaltered poems published for the first time.

16. GEORGE HERBERT (1593–1633)

Herbert was born into an accomplished aristocratic family and was a priest and poet, as well as a musician: he could play the lute, among other instruments. Born in Montgomery, Wales, he dedicated his life to God at a young age. At sixteen, he wrote a letter to his mother containing two sonnets to let her know that through his poetry he would do exactly that. However, he first pursued a secular life, with two stints as a member of parliament, before, disillusioned, being ordained as a deacon. In 1630, he became a canon of Lincoln Cathedral. He married his stepfather's cousin Jane Danvers after a courtship of just three days, and went on to adopt two orphaned nieces. Herbert died in 1633 and his poems would have died with him had it not been for the sound judgement of his friend, the scholar and deacon Nicholas Ferrar. Herbert had left it up to Ferrar to decide whether his work was worth publishing; if not, Herbert said, Ferrar should consign his poems to the fire. They were published as *The Temple,* the book King Charles I read for consolation in the final hours before his execution in 1649. Herbert was buried in Bemerton, near Salisbury, where he had become a rector.

17. MARY OLIVER (1935–2019)

Oliver was brought up in what she described as 'pastoral' countryside in Ohio and later adopted New England as her home. She had a lifelong passion for solitary walks in the wild, and along the Cape Cod coast, which inspired much of her poetry. She once found herself walking in the woods without a pen; cross that she could not note down her poetic thoughts, she returned to hide pencils in the trees so that in future she would not be at a loss. Oliver was notoriously reticent about her private life; her partner for forty years was the photographer Molly Cook, who was also her literary agent. She described her own family as dysfunctional and revealed in a 2011 interview that she had been abused as a child. Writing, she said, helped her create her own world.

18. CHARLES MACKAY (1814–1889)

Mackay was a Scottish poet, writer, editor and journalist. Born in Perth, he was brought up mainly by foster parents after his mother's death, and was partly educated in Brussels where he became fluent in French, German, Italian and Spanish. He initially supported himself by teaching Italian. He contributed poetry and articles to several newspapers, including both the *Morning Chronicle* and the *Daily News*, established by his associate and contemporary Charles Dickens. Mackay's *Voices from the Crowd* was published in 1846 and established his reputation as an astute critic of social and financial history. His study of the dangers of market speculation, *Extraordinary Popular Delusions and The Madness of Crowds*, was published in 1852 and is regarded as a classic text on human behaviour even today. Mackay visited America in the 1850s and returned there during the American Civil War as a correspondent for *The Times*. He published his autobiography *Through the Long Day* two years before his death.

19. RUTH PITTER (1897–1992)

Born in Ilford, Essex, the daughter of two teachers, Pitter was encouraged at Sunday family gatherings to recite poems learnt by heart the preceding week. She described herself as 'rural by adoption', citing the woodlands where she walked as a child as a key influence on her poetry. A bohemian, she ran her own furniture business, which specialised in painted decorative furniture – she was particularly skilled at flower-painting – and published eighteen volumes of poetry. Her business was bombed during World War II and Pitter went to work in a munitions factory, before moving to the country in the 1950s, where she gardened and lived quietly with her business partner and friend Kathleen O'Hara. Her collection of poems *A Mad Lady's Garland*, with a preface by her friend Hilaire Belloc, established her reputation. Pitter also cultivated a close friendship with C.S. Lewis, who encouraged her to embrace the Anglican faith. 'Did I tell you I'd taken to Christianity?' she wrote in a letter in 1948. 'I was driven to it by the pull of C.S. Lewis and the push of misery.'

20. SUSAN COOLIDGE (1835–1905)

Susan Coolidge was the pen name of Sarah Chauncey Woolsey, an American writer born into a wealthy, influential New England family (her uncle was the president of Yale). Coolidge was a nurse during the American Civil War; towards its end, she began writing. She also edited the letters and diaries of Fanny Burney, the eighteenth-century English writer. Coolidge wrote a series of children's books called *What Katy Did*, based on her own family. She lived in a book-lined house in Newport, Rhode Island, and died aged seventy.

21. JOHN MILTON (1608–1674)

The son of a composer, Milton was a poet, writer and statesman. He published his first book of poems – paraphrases of the Psalms – when he was just fifteen. His masterpiece was *Paradise Lost* (1663), written in ten volumes, and depicting Satan's war against God and Adam and Eve's expulsion from the Garden of Eden. *The Oxford English Dictionary* credits Milton with the first known use of many words that have entered the English language, including 'debauchery', 'lovelorn', 'disregard' and 'pandemonium' (used as the name for the capital of Hell in the poem). When he was thirty, Milton travelled to France and Italy and met the astronomer and physicist Galileo. His return to England during the Civil War prompted his career as a political writer. He was rewarded for his support of Oliver Cromwell and the execution of King Charles I with his appointment as Cromwell's 'Secretary for Foreign Tongues' in 1649. His job was to translate (mainly into Latin) official communications from the English government to other countries, and then to translate the replies back into English. After Cromwell's death, Milton was imprisoned for his role in the fall of Charles I and support for the Commonwealth, but released after a few months. Despite being blind by 1652, Milton continued to write until his death in 1674.

22. OSCAR HAMMERSTEIN II (1895–1960)

A theatre producer, director and prolific lyricist, co-writing 850 songs, Hammerstein was born in New York into a theatrical family and went by the nickname 'Ockie'. His mother died when he was just fifteen, then four years later, in 1914, his father (who persuaded him to study Law) died, leaving him dependent on his more theatrically inclined family members. Hammerstein and his collaborator, composer Richard Rodgers, went on to write some of the most popular musicals of the twentieth century, including *Oklahoma!* and *The Sound of Music*. When he died aged sixty-five, the lights of Times Square were turned off for one minute, and the lights in London's West End were dimmed.

23. JAMES WRIGHT (1927–1980)

Born in Martins Ferry, Ohio, Wright came from a part-Irish family – he once said that he had to watch out for being too garrulous, given his roots. He had an unhappy childhood. His father worked for fifty years in a glass factory; his mother left school at fourteen to work in a laundry. When he was sixteen, he suffered a nervous breakdown and subsequently missed a year of high school. Wright went on to join the army, being stationed in Japan during the American occupation in 1946. After studying back in America, he married and became a university lecturer. Wright's poetry was influenced by the suffering and poverty he had seen in his youth, his poems voicing his political and social concerns, especially the lot of the disenfranchised poor in the Midwest. Wright suffered from depression and alcoholism his entire life and ended one poem with the line, 'I have wasted my life.' He died in New York City in 1980 and is now regarded as one of America's finest twentieth-century poets.

24. VIOLET NEEDHAM (1876–1967)

Violet Needham was from a privileged and cosmopolitan background. Born in London's Mayfair, she was the daughter of Captain Charles Needham, 1st Lifeguards, whose nickname was 'Blastofino', and his Dutch wife, whose family had made a fortune out of tin concessions in the Dutch East Indies. Concealed beneath the veneer of Mayfair respectability was the fact that Captain Needham was a gambler. Needham recounted how their lifestyle switched from affluence to (comparative) poverty, depending on his success, and many of the heroines in her novels are rescued from precarious financial situations. When Needham and her sister Evelyn were nineteen and twenty respectively, their father was posted to Rome. They spent the next six years leading the same social life as young ladies in that privileged golden evening of the aristocracy all over Europe. Violet remained urban and stylish in appearance and habits, with beautiful (if, by the end of her life, outmoded) clothes, smoking Turkish cigarettes in a special holder. The Needham family returned to England permanently in 1902, and Violet became friends with Douglas William Freshfield, an explorer and alpinist. Needham began to tell bed-time stories to her nephews, which became the adventures of her character Dick Fauconbois, known as the Stormy Petrel. *The Black Riders* was eventually published in 1939. Early in the 1950s Violet gave up her London house and moved permanently to Gloucestershire to join her sister, who had long been widowed. Devoted to her sister, she died when she was ninety-one. Her published career as a writer had not begun until she was over sixty, and she produced nineteen books in eighteen years.

25. EDWARD THOMAS (1878–1917)

Born to Welsh parents in Lambeth, London, Thomas made his name during his life as a prose writer rather than a poet. He reviewed books for a living and wrote biographies as well as works of natural history, sometimes producing as many as three books a year. Unsatisfied by work that he felt was uncreative, and under constant financial pressure, Thomas endured recurrent psychological breakdowns as well as poor health. He only wrote poetry during the last three years of his life, encouraged by his friendship with American poet Robert Frost (Frost's most famous poem, 'The Road Not Taken', was inspired by walks with Thomas, and the latter's indecisiveness about which route to take). Thomas's poetry focused on rural England – he lived in Kent and Hampshire as an adult – and the way modern life can break up communities. Thomas joined the army in 1915, although as a mature married man he could have avoided enlisting. His poetry through this period alternates between recollections of his beloved countryside and meditations on the changes wrought by war, and what it was doing to everything he loved, as well as touching on his depression. In a poem written in January 1915, he tells us that at that time he was 'happy sometimes' but suffered 'a heavy body and a heavy heart'. He was killed in action at the battle of Arras in 1917.

26. ELIZABETH GASKELL (1810–1865)

Born in Chelsea, London, Gaskell was brought up by her aunt in the town of Knutsford (later the inspiration for her novel *Cranford*) near Manchester, after her mother had died. She spent years not seeing her father, and lacked a sense of financial security or a secure home. She is known as a novelist who explores the squalor and ills of industrial England in works such as *Mary Barton*, *Cranford*, *North and South* and *Wives and Daughters*. Friendly with other important writers of the time such as John Ruskin and Charlotte Brontë, she was an influence on Charles Dickens, who invited her to write for his magazine *Household Words*. His *Hard Times* was partly inspired by Gaskell's work. Lively and attractive, she married the Reverend William Gaskell. When their fifth child and only son Willie died of scarlet fever at nine months, she began writing to distract herself from her grief. Observing the inequality and hardship that came with industrialisation and the growth of factories, Gaskell's novel *North and South*, published in 1854, reflected her humanitarian ideals. While 'Mrs Gaskell' sounds matronly and safe, many of her views were radical, as were her criticisms of Victorian England. At the request of Charlotte Brontë's father Patrick, Gaskell published *The Life of Charlotte Brontë* in 1857. She died suddenly aged fifty-five while in Hampshire, a trip made in secret to buy a house with which she planned to surprise her husband and family.

Summer Writers

27. R. S. THOMAS (1913–2000)

Recognised as one of Wales's leading poets, Ronald Stuart Thomas was born in Cardiff. As the son of a sailor he was brought up in Holyhead and various other British ports; his father was often away at sea. He remained focused on Wales all his life and was known for his resistance to any colonisation of Wales by England, though he read his poems in the voice of a weary, upper-class Englishman. He studied Classics and Theology before he was ordained as an Anglican priest in 1937. His parishes included a mining village and several Welsh hill-farming communities. All his poems are imbued with religious themes, many of them bleak. He himself said that Christ was a poet and the New Testament was full of poetry. His artist wife Mildred encouraged him to write: he said that her reputation as a painter spurred him on to win recognition as a poet. Thomas retired as a clergyman in 1978. He and his wife rejected many of the amenities of modern life, and moved into a tiny, unheated cottage in Sarn y Plas, on the coast in Snowdonia. Free from the constraints of being a priest, he became a fierce advocate of Welsh nationalism, although he never supported Plaid Cymru because they recognised England's Parliament and therefore, in his view, did not go far enough in opposition to England. He was once described by the former Archbishop of Canterbury Robert Runcie as a 'tidy, boney man, with a thin face rutted by severity. And the poems are the man. Austere and simple and of repressed power.'

28. DAVID MASON (1954–)

Born in Bellingham, Washington, Mason is an American teacher, editor and poet who left Colorado College to become a fisherman in Alaska (though he later resumed his studies). He also spent some time working as a gardener in Rochester, New York. In 1980, he and his first wife moved to Greece for a year, where he became a friend of the British travel writer and war hero Patrick Leigh Fermor; he retains an enduring love for Greece, its language and people. His 2010 memoir is entitled *News from the Village: Aegean Friends*. Mason has taught at various American universities and now lives in Colorado. He was appointed Colorado poet laureate in 2010, and often chooses to write about the landscape there. His maternal grandfather, a coalminer turned physician, is remembered as one of the last 'horse and buggy driver' doctors in the state.

29. KOBAYASHI ISSA (1763–1828)

Issa was the child of agricultural workers. Born Kobayashi Nobuyuki, a dreamer and considered a disappointment to his family: more prone to wandering about in the fields than he was interested in maintaining or reaping them. His mother died young, and when his father remarried and had another son, he felt even more of an outsider. He travelled to Edo, now Tokyo, where he studied the haiku form and took the pen name Issa, meaning 'cup of tea'. He had a tough life, full of loss: legal battles for his inheritance, financial insecurity, the death of his four children in infancy and that of his wife in childbirth. But he found consolation in Shinto Buddhism and managed to produce a staggering volume of work (as well as visual art) that often seems positively sprung with joy and humour; his output of 20,000 haiku is ten times what Bashō managed. For all his insistence that the joys of life are fleeting, and his belief that we should free ourselves from attachment to material things and vanity about our works, his own work has survived two hundred years and brought happiness to many.

30. WILLIAM CULLEN BRYANT (1794–1878)

Born into a Calvinist, liberal and forward-thinking but impoverished family in the small village of Cummington, Massachusetts, Bryant was first encouraged to write poetry by his father, a surgeon and early advocate of homeopathy who had fallen on hard times, and who also wrote verse. The young boy was inspired in his literary aspirations by the beauty of the surrounding New England countryside, delighting in its brooks and rolling fields. He developed a love of language, influenced partly by the sermons he heard at church. He would construct a makeshift pulpit out of the parlour furniture and deliver sermons himself, in imitation of those he had heard. At just sixteen, he wrote the poem 'Thanatopsis' (Greek for 'a view of death'), in which, despite his religious upbringing, he said there was no heaven or hell (though he later modified this view). Published in 1817, the poem established a literary reputation which was to last throughout his long life. Despite his early poetic prowess as a teenager, he went on to train as a lawyer; it was a profession to which he had a lifelong aversion, but he never forgot the poverty of his upbringing and worried that poetry would not pay the bills. He later became a journalist and was a long-time editor of the *New York Evening Post*, where he promoted free trade, working men's rights, free speech, and a belief in the abolition of slavery. He once wrote that the most beautiful poetry 'is that which takes the strongest hold of the feelings... The great spring of poetry is emotion.' When Bryant died after a fall in 1878, New York went into mourning for one of its most respected men of letters.

31. ELIZABETH BARRETT BROWNING (1806–1861)

One of eleven children, Elizabeth Barrett Browning was brought up at the Hope End estate in Herefordshire, the daughter of a wealthy country squire, and was known by the nickname 'Ba'. Exceptionally erudite, she began to compose verses at the age of four: two years later she received from her father for 'some lines on virtue penned with great care' a ten-shilling note enclosed in a letter addressed to 'the Poet-Laureate of Hope End'. She was dogged with ill-health for much of her life. She suffered too from the drowning in 1840 of her favourite brother, the greatest sorrow of her life. The family moved to 50 Wimpole Street, where Barrett Browning remained mostly in her room for five years. Protected from the outside world and leading a bookish, upper-middle-class life surrounded by a loving family, Barrett Browning resumed her literary career, which had been partially interrupted during her serious illness. Soon she was acclaimed as one of Britain's most brilliant poets. Part of her literary reputation was based on her efforts to redress many forms of social injustice; in her poems and letters, she tackled issues such the slave trade, child labour, the mines and the mills of England, and the restrictions forced upon women in nineteenth-century society. Her work found its way into the home of fellow poet Robert Browning. Less successful, and six years younger than Barrett, he was full of energy, fashionable, and loved dining with the leading figures of the literary world. Elizabeth Barrett fell in love and began writing poems to him. The Brownings selected the ambiguous title 'Sonnets from the Portuguese', as if they were translations, to disguise the biographical significance of Elizabeth's love sonnets. Following their secret wedding, Elizabeth's father disinherited her and the couple moved to Florence.

32. GRACE NICHOLS (1950–)

The daughter of a headmaster, Grace Nichols was born in Georgetown, Guyana, where she grew up in a small country village on the coast. She has often credited her father for her love of books: she would dip into his library, which included work by Keats, Wordsworth and Shakespeare. She worked as a journalist and teacher before she moved the UK in 1977. In 1983 she published *I Is a Long Memoried Woman*, which won a Commonwealth poetry prize. Telling the story of an enslaved African woman taken to the Caribbean, it was later made into a film. She has written about the photographer Dora Maar – who remains known for being Picasso's lover, model and muse – and the story of the Caribbean itself. She is also a novelist, and has written poetry collections for children touching on, among other themes, stories of Guyanese folklore. She is a Vice-President of The Royal Society of Literature and currently lives in Sussex with her husband, the poet John Agard. She usually works through several drafts, writing by hand, though she says some poems come as gifts 'and you don't have to change a thing'.

33. E.E. CUMMINGS (1894–1962)

Cummings's full name was Edward Estlin Cummings, but he was always called Estlin. He is known for the absence of punctuation in his poetry, and he signed his name with both capital and lower-case double e. His trademark lack of a space after a comma began when he was fourteen; as a boy, he wrote a poem a day. He was the son of a Harvard professor, and was born in the first house in Cambridge, Massachusetts to have a wind-up telephone. His radicalism reflected the avant-garde circles in which he mixed at the start of the 1920s, when he lived in New York and Paris and enjoyed friendships with other experimental poets like Ezra Pound. He also painted, drawing inspiration from the Impressionist and Cubist movements. Cummings lived a bohemian life, drinking whisky sours, living in Greenwich Village in New York, frequenting burlesque and strip-tease shows and writing erotic verse. Despite this he was a staunch Republican and anti-communist, refusing an invitation to the White House from First Lady Jacqueline Kennedy because she was a Democrat. He was married twice, but his first love was the Parisian prostitute Marie-Louise Lallemand, whom he met in 1917 during World War I when he served as an ambulance driver (considering himself a pacifist). Cummings addressed Lallemand in his poems, love letters and drawings, writing to her in French.

34. GERARD MANLEY HOPKINS (1844–1889)

See earlier entry

35. WILLIAM BUTLER YEATS (1865–1939)

Yeats was born into the Protestant, Anglo-Irish class that controlled Ireland at the time, though his father was an artist and a rather ineffectual lawyer, and his family did not enjoy any political influence. He staunchly affirmed his Irish nationality. Many of his poems reflect Irish legends, ballads, folklore, settings and heroes, and he has become synonymous with Irish literature, to the point that his poetry appears in Irish passports. Born in Sandymount, Dublin, Yeats was initially educated at home by his mother, who entertained the family with Irish folktales and stories. Although he lived in London for much of his childhood, and again as an adult, he spent his holidays in County Sligo, where the tiny uninhabited island of Innisfree inspired one of his most famous poems – 'The Lake Isle of Innisfree', featured on page 118. He also had a longstanding interest in magic, mysticism and spirituality, and in 1890 he joined the Order of the Golden Dawn, a secret society that practised ritual magic. He once wrote that mystical life was 'at the centre of all that I do and all that I think and all that I write'. Many of his poems are inspired by the love of his life, the tall, beautiful Maud Gonne, who encouraged him in his support for Irish nationalism. Though he proposed to Maud, she turned him down – as, years later, did her daughter Iseult. He eventually married 25-year-old Georgie Hyde-Lees when he was fifty-two. During the first decade of the twentieth century, he was involved in running the Abbey Theatre company in Dublin, which he had co-founded in 1904; he also wrote plays for it, some influenced by the Japanese Noh tradition in which actors are story-tellers who convey meaning through their visual appearance and use of movement and dance. In 1922, he became a senator for the new Irish Free State, arguing against a ban on divorce and new censorship laws. Though a patriot, he deplored the bigotry and hatred that he detected in Ireland's nationalist movement. He died in 1939, in the south of France, but is buried in County Sligo.

36. WILLIAM WORDSWORTH (1770–1850)

Wordsworth was born in Cockermouth, Cumberland (though now known as Cumbria), in the Lake District, a landscape that he loved and with which he is strongly associated. Wordsworth was one of the founders of Romanticism, which covers a range of developments in art, literature, music and philosophy, spanning the late eighteenth and early nineteenth centuries. It emphasised the importance of the individual, the healing power of the imagination, and the notion that people should follow their ideals and authentic personal feelings. The intellectuals and poets who embraced it – such as Wordsworth, Blake, Coleridge, Shelley and Keats – challenged the establishment, inspired by a desire for liberty and horror at the exploitation of the poor. Wordsworth was hugely fond of walking, by night as well as by day (even though he apparently had no sense of smell to enjoy the flowers) and roamed Europe on foot in his early twenties before settling in the Lake District, where he lived with his sister Dorothy. Its landscape inspired much of his poetry, producing the mantra 'let nature be thy teacher'. In 1795, Wordsworth met the poet Samuel Taylor Coleridge in Somerset. Together they went on to write *Lyrical Ballads*, published in 1798. He famously described poetry in his introduction to the Ballads as 'the spontaneous overflow of powerful feelings' that 'takes its origin from emotion recollected in tranquillity'.

37. PAUL LAURENCE DUNBAR (1872–1906)

One of the first influential poets of colour in America, Dunbar was born in Dayton, Ohio, to freed slaves from Kentucky, and was the only African American in his class at school. Initially he hoped for a career in the law, but his widowed mother's finances meant he could not afford university. He was rejected for various jobs because of his race, settling for work as an elevator operator, a job that allowed him time to write. He went on to write novels, plays and lyrics, many of which express the plight of African Americans, as well as their accomplishments. He was acclaimed for verse written in the patois of the deep American South, but much of his work is also written in standard English. The 1903 musical comedy, *In Dahomey,* featured lyrics written by Dunbar and was the first all African-American musical. Despite his many successes, he suffered from alcoholism and depression. He relied on whisky to temper his chronic coughing but died of tuberculosis aged thirty-three, in his mother's arms, reciting the 23rd psalm.

38. SAPPHO (C630–C570 BC)

The Ancient Greek poet Sappho was a member of a noble family from the island of Lesbos, located off the coast of Turkey. Around 600 BC she and her family were exiled to Syracuse in Sicily. Little about her life is known for certain, but study of the remaining fragments of her poetry, as well as classical sources that mention her, imply that she would have presided over the rites of religious cults dedicated to pagan goddesses such as Aphrodite and Artemis. While doing this, Sappho may have written poetry for the performance of rites, or at weddings, or for a private, exclusively female audience of her disciples, to whom she may have also taught poetry. She commanded a respect across the Greek world that was equalled only by that given to Homer. In her poems, the speaker is usually a woman, and often expresses love and desire for other women (the words Sapphic and lesbian are derived from her name and her place of birth). Her sexuality was accepted in her own day but subsequent generations of readers from the pagan Romans and early Christians onwards have sought to either demonise or erase this aspect of her poetry. This may be one of the reasons for the lack of care taken in preserving her works, though new fragments of her poetry emerge from time to time, sometimes discovered in ancient caches of papyri.

39. MIMI KHALVATI (1944–)

Born in Tehran, Mimi Khalvati grew up on the Isle of Wight, and trained as an actor at Drama Centre London. She also attended SOAS to relearn the Persian she forgot as a child in English boarding schools, and later worked for a theatre company in Tehran, translating English scripts. Khalvati became a poet in middle age and, by her own admission, entirely by accident. She signed up to an Arvon Foundation course that she believed was for aspiring scriptwriters – something more in line with her previous dramatic training, which is in evidence at her melodic and powerful poetry readings. But the course turned out to be in poetry, and she decided to make the most of it anyway. It would be two years, though, before she would entirely commit her creative energies to poetry, at which point she was a single parent with two children, fitting in poetry workshops after finishing secretarial work for the day. Her debut collection, *In White Ink*, was published when she was forty-seven, and she has now published eight collections. As for the Arvon Foundation, whose poetry course she accidentally ended up taking, she is now a poetry tutor for them. She is also a poetry tutor for The Poetry School, which she founded. As a tutor, she advises students to beware of using potentially archaic words: she is said to have a particular dislike of the word 'beneath'.

Autumn Writers

40. EMILY BRONTË (1818–1848)

Best known for her novel *Wuthering Heights*, Brontë was brought up at the parsonage at Haworth in Yorkshire, the daughter of the Reverend Patrick Brontë and Maria Branwell Brontë, the fifth of their sixth children after Maria, Elizabeth, Charlotte and Branwell. She lost her mother when she was only three: nearly all the children in *Wuthering Heights* also become motherless. Her childhood was one of games, lessons, religious education and walks on the moors with her family. When she was six, she was sent with her sisters to Cowan Bridge school, where abuse was rife, the food was poor and the rooms cold, conditions that most likely hastened the deaths of Maria and Elizabeth, who both died of consumption in 1825. The three remaining sisters were afterwards educated at home. Brontë was known as an animal lover who befriended stray dogs or young rabbits. She closely observed birds, animals, plants and the changing skies, all of which inform a significant part of her poetry. At seventeen, she went back to school to Roe Head Girls' School, but a combination of homesickness and creative deprivation meant she returned home in October 1835. She forced herself to leave home again two more times, to teach at Law Hill and to study in Brussels, but then returned to Yorkshire for the rest of her life, where the moors remained an inspiration. Many of her poems were written on individual scraps of paper, in a tiny, crabbed script. In February 1844 Brontë began to copy her poems into two notebooks, one titled *Gondal*

Poems, the other left untitled. The act of copying itself suggests that Brontë took her poetry seriously and wanted it preserved. The only poems that were published in her lifetime were included in a slim volume by Brontë and her sisters Charlotte and Anne, titled *Poems by Currer, Ellis, and Acton Bell* (1846), which sold just two copies. Their pen names preserved their initials: Emily was Ellis Bell. She died in 1848, heartbroken at the death of her brother, so thin that her coffin measured only sixteen inches wide.

41. SUZI FEAY (DATE OF BIRTH UNDISCLOSED)

Suzi Feay first encountered poetry aged eight at Bolton School in Manchester, in the form of what she describes as Wordsworth's 'excruciating' poem 'We Are Seven'. She says it put her off poetry for years, but she got over it and now she says she even 'quite likes Wordsworth'. Aged ten she moved with her family to Burnley, where she grew up in the shadow of Pendle Hill and became enthralled by witches, ghosts and the supernatural. She studied English and Philosophy at Leeds University and began to review gigs for the local paper, documenting, for example, the first visit to the city of The Smiths, a band that went on to huge fame. Moving to London, she worked as journalist, spending five years at *Time Out* as a sub-editor and critic before moving to the books desk of the *Independent on Sunday* in 1994, where she eventually became Literary Editor. She has been a judge on many literary prize panels, and her poems have appeared in *Poetry Review, Magma* and the *London Magazine*. A regular broadcaster, she is a member of the Authors' Club and is currently President of The Critics' Circle.

42. JANE HIRSHFIELD (1953–)

Hirshfield was born in New York; her father was a clothing manufacturer and her mother a secretary. She graduated from Princeton as a member of the university's first graduating class to include women. She then studied for eight years at the San Francisco Zen Center. 'I felt that I'd never make much of a poet if I didn't know more than I knew at that time about what it means to be a human being,' Hirshfield once said. 'I don't think poetry is based just on poetry; it is based on a thoroughly lived life.' Many of her poems speak of the environment and social justice issues, what she calls 'unceasing wars'. Perhaps the best description of Hirshfield is as a woman of letters. She is the author of essays, anthologies and translations, especially of Japanese, drawing attention to the 31-syllable Japanese poetic form known as tanka. Though never a full-time academic, Hirshfield has also taught at American universities including the University of San Francisco and the University of Cincinnati. More recently, Hirshfield has been richly celebrated as a poet. In 2004, she received the Academy Fellowship from the Academy of American Poets. She currently lives in the San Francisco Bay area of California, and lists her hobbies as 'horses, gardening, and wilderness' and her religion as Zen Buddhist.

43. JULIA ABIGAIL FLETCHER CARNEY (1823–1908)

Julia Carney could not remember a time when she did not write poetry. When she was tiny, her older brothers and sisters would write down her rhymes before she was able to do so for herself. Her mother once forbade her to write any more poems but relented when she found her daughter's verses hidden in the attic. Born in Lancaster, Massachusetts, Carney's first poetry was published when she was fourteen. By the time she was seventeen, she was working as a teacher. Much of her work was set to music and sung as hymns – this musicality is clearly seen in her best-known poem 'Little Things'. It was written as a ten-minute writing assignment in a teacher's summer programme that she attended in Boston, and featured in generations of school textbooks. In 1849, she married a minister, Thomas J. Carney; they had nine children, losing four of them in infancy. She wrote for a wide variety of magazines and journals, using different pen names to fill her various columns, including Minnie May, Frank Fisher, Sadie Sensible and Minister's Wife: she preferred anonymity when she wrote critical pieces, such as those highlighting relationships between some ministers and their flocks. She was widowed in 1871 when her husband was thrown from a horse. Neighbours remembered her as a little old woman with snow-white hair, sitting in a rocking chair on her porch, watching the local children play.

44. JERICHO BROWN (1976–)

Brown was born Nelson Demery III in Shreveport, Louisiana, to parents who made their living cutting lawns and cleaning homes and other buildings. His family moved often; partly because of this disruption, Brown was expelled from school several times. He attributes his love of language to his mother, who would drop him and his sister at local libraries when she had to work; he has described the librarians as his babysitters. He attended Dillard University and the University of New Orleans, receiving his PhD from Houston. He has taught at many universities and worked as a speechwriter and press officer for the Mayor of New Orleans's office, where he composed the response given after Hurricane Georges in 1998 and which he has described as a 'huge training ground'. In 2020 he received the Pulitzer Prize for Poetry for his latest collection *The Tradition*, from which 'Crossing' is taken. He is currently Director of the Creative

Writing Program at Emory University in Atlanta, a job he chose as he wanted to be closer to his Southern roots. He has called poetry a 'calling'. 'You do it whether you like it or not.' He has said, in multiple interviews, that the acts of reading and writing poetry have saved his life, and he has spoken openly about his struggles with suicidal thoughts from an early age, partly because he struggled with living life as a gay man. Jericho Brown is a pseudonym, chosen to separate him from his anti-gay evangelical upbringing. He has said he is addicted to *Game of Thrones*.

45. LOUISA LAWSON (1858–1920)

Lawson was born in New South Wales to a working-class family. She left school at thirteen and, after marrying a Norwegian miner who was often away working, raised their four children for the most part by herself. She left her husband when she was twenty-five and supported herself and her children by running cattle, sewing and managing a boarding house. This gave Lawson a first-hand experience of the inequality of nineteenth-century society, and how little control women were allowed over their own lives. After buying shares in a newspaper that she edited with her son, the poet Henry Lawson, she put together Australia's first magazine produced by women for women: *The Dawn*. In its first issue she wrote, under a pen name: 'There has hitherto been no trumpet through which the concentrated voice of womankind could publish their grievances and their opinions... Here then is *Dawn*, the Australian Woman's Journal and Mouthpiece.' Using this platform, she successfully campaigned for votes for women. She suffered much hardship throughout her life and was traumatised by the death of her daughter Tegan, whom she mourned for beautifully in her poem 'All's Well'. She died in an institution after a prolonged period of mental illness.

46. RAYMOND CARVER (1938–1988)

The son of a heavy-drinking sawmill worker father and a waitress mother, Carver was born in Clatskanie, Oregon. In his first job he worked alongside his father. By the time he was twenty, he was married with two children and working variously as a janitor, petrol-station attendant and delivery man, which he combined with writing poems and short stories, and attending creative writing courses. His pieces about the working poor mirrored his own life. His wife supported his career, and Carver himself continued to combine his writing with other employment, working for a subsidiary of IBM in California and as a university lecturer. During his years of working at these miscellaneous jobs, writing and raising children, Carver started abusing alcohol and his marriage broke up. In the late 1970s, Carver fell in love with poet Tess Gallagher, who became his muse. After being hospitalised three times in 1976 and 1977, he stopped drinking with the help of Alcoholics Anonymous. The couple moved to Syracuse, New York, where they both taught at the university. Their house became so popular that they hung a sign outside saying 'Writers at Work', in order to be left alone. Controversy arose recently after it was revealed that his long-time editor had significantly changed many of Carver's early stories. He died at home of lung cancer when he was fifty. Six weeks earlier he had married Tess.

47. DEREK WALCOTT (1930–2017)

Walcott was born on the isolated volcanic island of St Lucia in the West Indies, of African and European descent. He originally trained as a painter, before finding fame as a poet and playwright: he founded two theatres, one in Boston and one in Trinidad. His father died when he was young; his mother was a seamstress and schoolteacher who helped finance the self-publication of his first collection of poetry, which he sold on street corners when he was nineteen. He was educated at the University of the West Indies, Jamaica, and worked as a reviewer, academic, art critic, painter and playwright. In 1981, he was hired by Boston University and taught literature there for two decades, as well as at Columbia, Yale, and Essex University in England. His prose and poetry explored the Caribbean cultural experience, its joys as well as the scars of colonialism, and he sometimes used Caribbean patois as well as standard English. He was married with three children. In 2009, he was touched by scandal when an accusation of sexual harassment drove him to withdraw his candidacy for the Oxford Professorship of Poetry, though many of his colleagues supported him.

48. PORTIA NELSON (1920–2001)
The youngest of nine children, born into a Mormon family, Nelson grew up on a farm in Brigham City, Utah. She was multi-talented: a poet, singer, songwriter and actress. In the 1950s, she performed in the thriving cabaret scene, famous for her elegant figure and silvery soprano voice. Relatively late on in her career, she played the cantankerous nun Sister Berthe in the 1965 movie version of *The Sound of Music*. This set the precedent for her appearing in two other films as a nun. In 1977, she published her book of writings, *There's a Hole in my Sidewalk: The Romance of Self-Discovery*, and continued to sing and act.

49. FRED D'AGUIAR (1960–)
Fred D'Aguiar was born in London to Guyanese parents and moved to Guyana for the duration of his early childhood to live with his grandparents, due in part to his parents' financial difficulties. Living in a post-colonial country during the 1960s, the young D'Aguiar

witnessed racial tension and political violence. He came back to London at the age of twelve. He trained and worked as a psychiatric nurse for three years while reading and writing in his spare time, then went to Kent University. He graduated in 1985, and his debut collection *Mama Dot* was published the same year. He won the Whitbread First Novel award for 1994's *The Longest Memory*. Much of D'Aguiar's work is preoccupied with the legacy of slaves and their descendants in the global diaspora. His poem 'Tidal' builds on fragments of information about the lives of slaves in England from hundreds of years ago. 'Bloodlines' (2000), written in the same metrical form as Lord Byron's poem 'Don Juan', chronicles the nineteenth-century romance of the son of a plantation owner and an enslaved black woman who run away together. His 2009 'Continental Shelf' grappled with the shootings at Virginia Tech, where he was teaching at the time. Yet despite the darkness of much of his subject matter, interviewers describe D'Aguiar in person as outgoing, engaging and humorous. D'Aguiar describes himself as 'at bottom a cheerful person', something he attributes in part to his children (he has two). 'With kids, they force you go get out of bed. They force you to smile. They remind you of spontaneity. So I always check my bad mood and my dystopic vision at the door.' He is currently at UCLA, directing its Creative Writing Programme.

50. INUIT PRAYER

'Inuit' means 'the people', and refers to communities living in the Arctic, as well as in parts of Quebec, Alaska and Russia. In some areas, Inuit people are called Eskimos, but many Inuit people now find this term offensive. In the past, Inuit lived in round houses made of blocks of snow known as igloos, while in the Summer they lived in tent-like huts made of animal skins stretched over a frame.

To travel across the snow, the Inuit used sleds pulled by dogs, typically huskies, while small boats or kayaks were used for hunting on the waters of the Arctic.

51. CHARLOTTE BRONTË (1816–1855)

Though much of her life was marked by tragedy, Brontë wrote novels and poems that found great success in her lifetime. The eldest of the three Brontë sisters, all of whom wrote classics of English literature, Charlotte was born in Thornton, in the wilderness of the Yorkshire moors, and raised in a parsonage. Her mother died when Charlotte was five, leaving six young children in the care of her husband, the Reverend Patrick Brontë. Charlotte began writing poetry and stories as a child, sometimes about her hero the Duke of Wellington, and with her talented siblings created magazines that included essays, letters and advertisements, as well as notes from the editor. Her sister Emily (see entry page 206) wrote *Wuthering Heights*, while Charlotte is best-known for writing *Jane Eyre*, published in 1847 to instant success. She based Lowood, the fictional school in the novel, on the one that she attended with her sisters. For an adult, Brontë was tiny, around four foot seven, about which she was self-conscious. She worked as a teacher and governess, professions she hated: she once wrote about the misery of 'having the charge given me of a set of pampered, spoilt, and turbulent children, whom I was expected constantly to amuse as well as instruct'. When she was twenty, she sent some of her poems to the English Poet Laureate Robert Southey, who wrote back saying that 'literature cannot be the business of a woman's life...' Shy and secretive, she kept her writing from her father and used the male pseudonym Currer Bell when she first published *Jane Eyre*. Having rejected various other proposals, she finally married the Reverend

Nicholls in 1854. She died less than a year later at just thirty-eight, while pregnant.

52. MAX EHRMANN (1872–1945)

Ehrmann was an American writer, poet and lawyer. Indiana-born and Methodist-raised, he was one of five children of German immigrants, and was never part of the poetry establishment. His parents had emigrated from Bavaria in the 1840s and had a woodworking business. The three older Ehrmann brothers went into business, but Max once wrote that he resolved 'not to embrace the conventional aim of life', which was to 'become rich'. Ehrmann went to Harvard to study Philosophy and Law, after which he moved back to Indiana, where he served as deputy state attorney for two years, then worked at his brothers' overalls factory. He simultaneously wrote plays and poems, and published books and pamphlets. After ten years, he left work to concentrate on his writing, and his family supported him. He is best known for his 1927 prose poem 'Desiderata', which he wrote when he was fifty-five. Shortly after finishing the poem in 1927, Ehrmann sold autographed prints and cards of the poem. A bachelor for most of his life, in June 1945 he married Bertha Pratt King, a Smith College graduate and suffragette, before his death three months later.

ACKNOWLEDGEMENTS

My thanks to my agent Elizabeth Sheinkman for her wise counsel, kindness and editorial judgement as well as to Liz Gough, my brilliant editor at Yellow Kite. Liz and I worked together on my memoir *Black Rainbow* and it is lovely to be reunited with her for a second book that celebrates poetry. It would have been impossible to sort all the copyright permissions involved in this book without the help of Beth Dufour and Tracy Latimer. Thank you to Oliver Martin for all his work on publicity. I have been fortunate too in all the editorial input and professional assistance from Liv Nightingall at Yellow Kite, alongside Sally Somers. Thanks also to my family, especially my sister Rosanna Gardner, my brother-in-law Anthony Gardner, my late mother Linda Kelly, and my husband Sebastian Grigg for all their poetic suggestions, support and encouragement. As always, the home team of Elena Langtry, Tara Maxwell and Emma Russell kept the show on the road. I am grateful to the expert anthologist Kate Kavanagh for sharing her enthusiasm for poetry and reading the book as well as editorial improvements and thoughts from Alan Jenkins and Edna Pottersman, and introductions to poems from Izabella Karinsky-Stanley, and Jonathan McAloon. Especial gratitude to Eliza Hoyer-Millar who has believed in this book from its outset and helped me every step of the way. And finally, my appreciation to all those who have shared poems and their thoughts over the years in my Healing Words workshops. This book wouldn't have happened without you.

CREDITS, COPYRIGHT AND PERMISSIONS

Stevie Smith, 'Not Waving but Drowning' from *Collected Poems of Stevie Smith* © Stevie Smith 1972. Reprinted by permission of Faber and Faber Ltd.

F. Scott Fitzgerald, from *The Crack-Up*, 1945.

John Berryman, 'He Resigns' from *Collected Poems 1937–1971* © Kate Donahue Berryman 1988. Reprinted by permission of Farrar, Straus and Giroux. All rights reserved.

Abraham Lincoln, from a letter to John T. Stuart, 1841, included in *The Collected Works of Abraham Lincoln*, Rutgers University Press, 1953.

Gerard Manley Hopkins, 'No Worst, There Is None' from *Poems* 1918.

John Clare, 'I Am', 1848.

Pele Cox, 'Afterwards,' © Pele Cox. Reproduced with permission of Pele Cox.

Traditional spiritual, 'Sometimes I Feel Like a Motherless Child'.

Helen Waddell (translator), 'Accidie' from *The Desert Fathers* (1936). Reproduced with permission from L. Anson and the Estate of Helen Waddell.

Anne Sexton, 'The Sickness Unto Death' from *The Awful Rowing Toward God* © Linda Gray Sexton and Loring Conant, Jr. 1981. Reprinted by permission of SLL/Sterling Lord Literistic, Inc.

Johann Wolfgang von Goethe, 'Who Ne'er his Bread in Sorrow Ate, translated by Henry Wadsworth Longfellow.

Tishani Doshi, 'Dog in the Valley' from *Everything Begins Elsewhere* (2012). Reproduced with permission of Bloodaxe Books.

John Keats, 'Ode on Melancholy', 1819.

Matsuo Bashō, 'The Temple Bell Stops' translated by Robert Bly from *The Sea and The Honeycomb* © Robert Bly 1971. Reprinted by permission of Georges Borchardt, Inc., for the Estate of Robert Bly.

Emily Dickinson, '"Hope" is the thing with feathers', 1891.

George Herbert, 'Love', 1633.

Mary Oliver, 'Wild Geese' from *Dream Work* © Mary Oliver 1986. Reprinted by permission of Grove/Atlantic, Inc. Any third party use of this material, outside of this publication, is prohibited.

Charles Mackay, 'O Ye Tears!', 1865.

Ruth Pitter, 'For Sleep, or Death' from *Collected Poems* (2021). Reproduced with permission from Enitharmon Editions.

Susan Coolidge, 'New Every Morning' from *A Few More Verses* 1899.

John Milton, from 'Paradise Lost', 1667.

Oscar Hammerstein II, 'You'll Never Walk Alone' from *Carousel*, lyrics by Oscar Hammerstein II, music by Richard Rodgers © 1945 Williamson Music Company c/o Concord Music Publishing. Copyright renewed. All rights reserved. Reprinted by permission of Hal Leonard Europe Ltd.

James Wright, 'A Blessing' from *Collected Poems* © James Wright 1971. Reprinted with permission of Wesleyan University Press.

Violet Needham, from *The Black Riders*, Collins 1939.

Edward Thomas, 'The Unknown Bird' from *Collected Poems*, Faber 1979.

Elizabeth Gaskell, from *North and South*, 1854.

R. S. Thomas, 'The Bright Field' from *Collected Poems 1945–1990* © R. S. Thomas 1993. Phoenix 1993. Reprinted by permission of Orion Publishing Group.

David Mason, 'In the Mushroom Summer' from *The Hudson Review Vol LIX, No 2* (Summer 2006) © David Mason 2006. Reprinted with permission of *The Hudson Review*.

Kobayashi Issa, 'Step by Step' translated by Geoffrey Bownas and
   Anthony Thwaite from *The Penguin Book of Japanese Verse* (1964).
   Translation © Geoffrey Bownas and Anthony Thwaite 1964, 1998,
   2009. Reprinted by permission of Penguin Books Ltd.

William Cullen Bryant, 'The Gladness of Nature', 1853.

Elizabeth Barrett Browning, 'The Best Thing in the World' from *Last
   Poems*, 1862.

Grace Nichols, 'Advice on Crossing a Street in Delhi' from *Picasso, I Want
   My Face Back* (Bloodaxe Books) © Grace Nichols 2009. Reproduced
   with permissions from Curtis Brown Group Ltd on behalf of Grace
   Nichols.

E. E. Cummings, 'i thank You God for most this amazing', from
   Complete Poems: 1904–1962 (ed George Firmage) © 1950, 1978, 1991
   by the Trustees for the E. E. Cummings Trust © 1979 by George
   James Firmage. Reprinted by permission of Liveright Publishing
   Corporation.

Gerard Manley Hopkins, 'Pied Beauty', 1877, from *Poems*, 1918.

William Butler Yeats, 'The Lake Isle of Innisfree', 1888, published in the
   National Observer 1890.

William Wordsworth, from 'Tintern Abbey' from *Lyrical Ballads* 1798.

Paul Laurence Dunbar, 'A Summer's Night' from *The Complete Poems of
   Paul Laurence Dunbar*, Dodd, Mead, and Company 1913.

'Fragment' from Sappho, from *Sappho: Poems & Fragments*, translated by
   Josephine Balmer. Reproduced with permission of Bloodaxe Books.

Mimi Khalvati, 'Soapstone Retreat' from *The Meanest Flower* (Carcanet
   2007). Reprinted by permission of Carcanet.

Emily Brontë, 'Fall, Leaves, Fall' from *The Complete Poems of Emily Brontë*
   1910.

Suzi Feay, 'Revenant', printed with permission of Suzi Feay.

Jane Hirshfield, 'Lake and Maple' from *Each Happiness Ringed by Lions*
   (Bloodaxe Books 2005). Reprinted with permission of Bloodaxe Books.

Julia Abigail Fletcher Carney, 'Little Things', 1845.

Jericho Brown, 'The Crossing' from *The Tradition* (Picador Poetry 2019) © Macmillan. Reproduced with permission of the Licensor through PLSclear.

Louisa Lawson, 'A Reverie', 1903.

Raymond Carver, 'Happiness' from *Poetry Magazine*, The Wylie Agency 1985 ©Tess Gallagher 1989, reprinted by permission of the Wylie Agency (UK) Ltd.

Derek Walcott, 'Love After Love' from *Collected Poems 1948–1994* © Derek Walcott. Reprinted by permission of Faber and Faber Ltd.

Portia Nelson, 'Autobiography in Five Short Chapters' from *There's a Hole in My Sidewalk: The Romance of Self-Discovery* © Portia Nelson 1993. Reproduced with the permission of Beyond Words/Atria Books, a division of Simon & Schuster, Inc. All rights reserved.

Fred D'Aguiar, 'The Border' from *Letters to America* (Carcanet 2020) © David Higham Associates. Reprinted with permission of Carcanet.

Anon/Traditional, 'Life's a Journey', translated by William John Alexander Worster c.1921.

Charlotte Brontë, 'Life' from *Poems by Currer, Ellis, and Acton Bell* 1846.

Max Ehrmann, 'Desiderata' c.1921

ABOUT THE AUTHOR

Rachel Kelly is a writer and mental health campaigner. She shares her experience of depression and strategies that have helped her recover and is an advocate for the therapeutic power of poetry. She runs 'Healing Words' poetry workshops for charities, at festivals and in prisons, and has been a judge for the Koestler Poetry Prize and the Rethink Mental Illness Poetry Awards. Her memoir *Black Rainbow: How Words Healed Me: My Journey Through Depression* describes how poetry was an integral part of her recovery. Her books include *The Happy Kitchen*, *Walking on Sunshine* and *Singing in the Rain* and are published in over ten countries. A former *Times* journalist, Rachel is now an ambassador for charities including SANE, The Counselling Foundation, the Big Give and Head Talks. She lives in London with her husband and their children.

books to help you live a good life

Join the conversation and tell
us how you live a #goodlife

🐦 @yellowkitebooks

📘 YellowKiteBooks

📌 Yellow Kite Books

📷 YellowKiteBooks